The FURNACE of LEADERSHIP DEVELOPMENT

Tom,

I hope that you will find this book to be a useful leadership tool.

Rick

"The integrity of the upright will guide them..."

Proverbs 11:3

The FURNACE of LEADERSHIP DEVELOPMENT

How to Mold Integrity and Character in Today's World

RICK DAVIS

The Furnace of Leadership Development:
How to Mold Integrity and Character in Today's World

Published by JAVA HOUSE PUBLISHING
Loveland, Colorado

The content of this book has not been endorsed by the Loveland Fire Rescue Authority in Colorado, nor is it an official representation of Loveland Fire Rescue Authority policies or procedures. This book is the author's recollections of his experiences as he has recalled events, locations, and conversations from memory. In some cases, names and personal characteristics have been changed to ensure anonymity.

Library of Congress Control Number: 2019907328

DAVIS, RICK, Author
THE FURNACE OF LEADERSHIP DEVELOPMENT
RICK DAVIS

ISBN: 978-1-7330735-0-9

BUSINESS & ECONOMICS / Leadership
BIOGRAPHY & AUTOBIOGRAPHY / Fire & Emergency Services

Editing by Alexandra O'Connell, Your Resident Wordsmith
Cover Design by Nick Zelinger, NZ Graphics
Interior Design and Layout by Michelle M. White, MMW Books, LLC
Logo Design by Chelsea Hoffman, Easely Inspired

QUANTITY PURCHASES: Schools, companies, professional groups, clubs, and other organizations may qualify for special terms when ordering quantities of this title. For information, email Info@JavaHousePublishing.com.

Dedication

This book is dedicated to our firefighters, police officers, and EMS personnel who work tirelessly to protect us every day. The book is also dedicated to all of the members of the U.S. armed forces, past, present, and future. Without their sacrifice to secure and maintain our freedoms, this book would not be possible.

Table of Contents

Foreword

I am a lifelong student of leadership and I have a regrettable observation to make: Most modern leadership books are bad. Many are written either as esteem-soothing "self-help" therapy (*everyone can be a great leader!*) or as magical "shortcuts" to instant mastery (*the three tricks to rise to the top!*).

You might naturally ask: So, what's the problem with self-help and shortcuts? Nothing, if you're assembling a table you just bought at Ikea. Any hack easing the misery of furniture assembly is an unalloyed good in my mind.

But leadership is not a piece of furniture to be quickly assembled. Understood correctly, leadership is a master craft. As such, leadership excellence will take time—a lifetime, really.

So, you can imagine my delight when I read Rick Davis's book. As I turned each page, I thought: Here is an antidote to our society's mindless demand for instant gratification. Here is a book that stands firmly against the thin gruel of new-age gimmickry. Here is a book that returns *character* and *behavior* to their essential roles in determining true excellence and "a good life."

To say I was delighted with Rick's book should not imply I was surprised by its quality. I've known Rick for the past decade, sat in his firehouse and home, and I have learned, firsthand, of his integrity, keen intellect, and devotion to his profession.

Rick is an exemplar of the highest manifestation of leading, what I call "when the leader becomes the lesson." Here's what I mean: When we seek and attain mastery, our example is the teacher; our lives become the lesson. Who Rick has become as a man and leader, and how deep grooves were slowly etched in his character, are the essence of this book.

Beyond that, let me offer four other reasons to read this book:

- It's timely. Too many books promote a simplistic "to do" approach to leading. Well-intended, maybe, but essentially useless. Rick instead offers a soul-searching look into his life and reveals with penetrating candor the peaks and vales of real leadership experience.
- It's readable. You'll feel like you're sitting across the table from Rick and having a discussion. Deep teaching is offered here, but it feels more akin to a trusted conversation where gems are passed across the table.
- It's truthful. Rick addresses the vexing elements of life, the highs and lows, and helps us understand that, in leadership, it is often "two steps forward and one step back," where paradoxically, it is often the backward step, the failure, which is most crucial for growth.
- It's spiritually uplifting. Rick gently reminds us that humans are always at our best when we align to something greater than ourselves. He points out that when we willingly genuflect to sturdy virtues and uphold a code of behavioral principles, we create strong moral centers in both leader and follower, citizen and city, teacher and student, parent and child.

This book is a welcome gift to me and all who follow the leader's journey. Rick helps us recall this ancient but necessary wisdom: Only experiences truly convert us; words seldom do. Our experiences—our wins, losses, and sacrifices—produce a crucible effect delivering the necessary heat to burn away our lesser selves and gradually reveal our essential excellence. There are simply no shortcuts.

What I've found to be true about real growth and improvement is this: we need to be reminded, more than told, what is right. Thank you, Rick, for this timely and wonderful reminder. Semper Fidelis.

— Paul Callan, Colonel USMC (Ret.)
Creator of The Callan Course on Leadership

Preface

Throughout the years, thousands of books, articles, and papers have been written about leadership. So why would I undertake the effort to author another book on the subject?

God has given me more than I could ever imagine. Including the opportunities to share with others my experiences, leadership perspective, and the many lessons I've learned. These opportunities have taken place with my family, one-on-one with friends and associates, in the classroom, at the scene of emergencies, and through countless cups of coffee at the fire station kitchen table. My motivation for writing is to extend the same opportunity to those whom I will never meet, while at the same time fulfilling my duty and responsibility to pass on the leadership lessons I've learned. It is my desire and intent for you to say, "Hey! I've wondered about similar problems, and now I have answers and guidance on what to do."

In March 1972, I found my father dead on the floor from a heart attack. Since then, my perspective has been shaped by years filled with ups and downs, happiness and sadness, excitement and disappointment, victory and defeat. By my roles as a student, an enlisted member of the military, an employee, an instructor, a firefighter, a battalion chief, and a husband and father. A perspective based on my training, education, and study of leadership. A perspective based on walking the battlefields of the American Revolution and the Civil War. A perspective based on countless conversations with others about leadership and human behavior.

These threads weave together to create a leadership tapestry. What is my responsibility with the tapestry? Do I neatly fold the cloth and place it in a closet for no one to see or use? Do I display the material at the county fair, hoping to win a blue ribbon prize? No.

I have a duty and responsibility to share the tapestry with other people so they can grow and develop into better leaders. My duty and responsibility are also interwoven with a biblical perspective found in Luke 12:48: "For everyone to whom much is given, from him much will be required; and to whom much has been committed, of him they will ask the more."

Join me in the neighborhood fire station, where you are greeted by the friendly faces and smiles of firefighters anxious to share their experiences and show you around. Walking toward the back of the station, you pass the shiny brass pole descending from the second floor. To your right, you see the large, red fire engine. You notice the firefighters' protective equipment neatly laid out next to the engine in preparation for a hasty departure. To your left, you look through the glass on the door and see the heart of the fire station: the kitchen. I invite you to sit with me at the firehouse kitchen table, drink a cup of coffee, and discuss leadership.

Introduction

Several years ago, I taught a leadership class at our church to a group of adult men and women. I asked how many leaders were in the room, and out of approximately fifty people, less than six raised their hands. I then asked how many parents, aunts, and uncles were present, and hands shot up across the room. To cap off the questions, I posed the following to everyone: "How many of you influence someone else in your life?" Again, everyone raised their hands.

Why was there such a disparity in the number of responses to the first question compared with the last two? The answer lies in the fact that all too often people believe leadership is associated with a title, rank, or position within an organization. In reality, leadership exists, thrives, and dies across a broad spectrum of the human race, and has nothing to do with title, rank, or position.

Unfortunately, some of the most incompetent people I have worked for over the years held a title, rank, or position of authority. They were incapable of leading a troop of Cub Scouts to a water fountain. On the other hand, I have worked for fantastic leaders who held higher rank than me.

It is important not to confuse a position of authority with leadership. Recently, in the small town of Severance, Colorado, a nine-year-old boy named Dana wanted to have snowball fights with his brother. However, if Dana and his brother threw snowballs at each other, they were breaking the law because of an archaic town ordinance. The courageous third-grade student approached the town board with the intent to change the law—and he was successful. At his age he possesses very little power beyond telling his dog to come, sit, lay down, shake, and speak. Yet he influenced a local government to change an arcane law.

Leadership is composed of integrity, trust, credibility, determination, and physical and moral courage. Leadership involves listening, consistency, justice, and equity. These and other qualities come into play when we deal with organizational monsters, intra-team conflict, bias toward others, and providing and receiving feedback. A key component of leadership is self-control over anger and negative emotional responses. How we handle disappointment, rejection, and failure also impacts our leadership of others. Leaders are decision-makers and have the ability to function in an environment of chaos. Another significant element of leadership not only involves our personal development but the development of those we influence and are responsible for.

I address each of these topics while incorporating my experiences from boyhood to the present. Some of these experiences are positive and others negative. There have been times when someone put an industrial belt sander to my rear end and I've learned lessons the hard way. We can learn from both types of lessons and apply them to our leadership growth. Following each chapter are short stories reinforcing the previously discussed material. Also, embedded within each chapter are Bible verses providing a spiritual perspective related to the various leadership issues.

Throughout the book, I use real names for real people involved in the examples and experiences that had a positive impact on me. However, in places I substitute fictitious names for real people in order to protect their privacy. You will be introduced to a character named Joe Schmuckatelli. Joe is familiar to any Marine and their friends and families. He's been around for a long time, and so far, I have not found anyone who can pinpoint when he was born. For Marines, Joe is often used to identify nondescript individuals or those of dubious character. I opted to use Joe as an ordinary individual and leave it to the reader's imagination as to what he looks like.

As you read, never lose sight of the fact that the key to leadership is *people*. Without people, there can be no leadership. These are the people in our lives: our families, spouses, loved ones, friends, coworkers, subordinates, casual acquaintances, and others we encounter on a daily basis. This leads to the often-debated question: Are leaders born or made? Yes. Leaders are both born *and* made. Each of us is born with a genetic code inherited from our parents. God has endowed us with a unique personality, individual traits, talents, gifts, and abilities. What happens with all of those is dependent on a number of factors, including our family, upbringing, education, experiences, and a wide range of other influences. But that is not the focus of the book.

Before delving into those topics and taking a closer look at them, I have several questions for you to consider:

- Do you struggle as a leader?
- Do you feel like you are the only person working through a leadership problem?
- Do you feel like you don't measure up as a leader?
- Have you stumbled and failed as a leader?
- Have you attended a class or read a book that leaves you with the impression that leadership is easy and a rosy path?
- Are you afraid to ask questions about leadership for fear your boss or subordinates may think less of you?
- Do you hold to the belief that leaders are only people with a title, rank, or position of authority?

If you are a normal human being, you probably answered *yes* to some or all of those questions. You may have come up with others which aren't part of the list. If this is the case, my reasons for writing *The Furnace of Leadership Development* are validated. You hold within your hands a tool that will help mold integrity and character in your life and make you a better leader. Join me now over a cup of coffee and enjoy the warmth of the brew while you allow the heat of the furnace to work in your life.

1 *But Gunny, Why Me!?* **The Foundation of Integrity**

"Therefore whoever hears these sayings of Mine, and does them, I will liken him to a wise man who built his house on the rock: and the rain descended, the floods came, and the winds blew and beat on that house; and it did not fall, for it was founded on the rock."

— Matthew 7:24-25

A common soil found in the State of Colorado is bentonite, a shifting, clay-like material. Building a house on bentonite requires extra precautions to ensure the stability of the foundation by drilling down to bedrock. A failure to follow sound construction procedures results in fractured walls, concrete basement floors cracking and separating from the foundation, and in some cases, basement walls pushing into the house by several feet. No one wants to live in a house with issues like that.

In Matthew 7, Jesus speaks of the wise man who built his house on a foundation of rock and the structure withstood the harsh elements and passage of time. In the verses that follow, Christ describes a man who built his house on sand. The house could not endure the howling wind, driving rain, or floods, and it collapsed. You do not need a degree in geology to understand that rock is solid and sand shifts. Likewise, leadership is built upon the rock-solid foundation of integrity. Anything less is unacceptable.

STRONG FOUNDATIONS

For most people, purchasing a house is a major financial investment. Would you be willing to enter into a thirty-year mortgage knowing that Joe Schmuckatelli and Sons took shortcuts to increase their profit margin? Would you sign the contract knowing your new house is on bentonite soil, but the shady contractors opted not to drill down to bedrock? Most likely you would be appalled and walk away from the deal. If you are like most people, you will then share your disgust with friends, relatives, coworkers, and anyone who will listen.

Schmuckatelli and Sons build houses on shaky foundations because they lack integrity. I do not want Joe building my house, and I do not want to work for someone like him, either. Yet the lack of integrity is pandemic in our world. It infects families, businesses, churches, athletics, nonprofit organizations, and all levels of government.

Webster's Dictionary describes integrity as an adherence to a code of values, soundness, and completeness. Furthermore, integrity is one of the Marine Corps leadership traits, defined as "the quality of absolute honesty, trustfulness, and uprightness of character and moral principles."[1] Integrity is doing what is right when others are willing to compromise their ethics to obtain a financial reward, promotion, or recognition. Integrity translates to a clean conscience, allowing ourselves to look into the mirror and also into the eyes of the people around us. Job 31:6 reads, "Let me be weighed on honest scales, That God may know my integrity."

We can look to the Marine Corps and see their core values of honor, courage, and commitment as an example to follow. I have learned that maintaining and protecting integrity and honor require a steadfast commitment backed by moral courage. Integrity did not automatically come with joining the Marine Corps or the Air Force. My parents instilled this in me at an early age by consistently teaching and reinforcing the importance of doing the right thing at all times, regardless of the consequences.

THE REWARDS OF INTEGRITY

Many people in supervisory positions have worked hard to get where they are. Yes, some seemingly rocket into these roles with little effort or through favoritism of one degree or another. However, I am not addressing that issue. I am writing to those who have dedicated the time, the determination, and the energy to be promoted or hired into supervision. You have taken tests, gone through interviews, or have been pulled aside by your boss and told that you are going to be a supervisor. In the military and fire service, promotions are earned through various testing processes. They are stressful and create a tremendous amount of anxiety. When you earn the promotion, you are not only excited, but you look forward to new assignments and challenges. Keep in mind, integrity will open doors, allowing opportunities that may stagger our greatest imaginations.

During my time in the Marine Corps, I achieved the rank of E-5, sergeant, and I enjoyed the responsibilities that came with the position. Initially I entered the Marine Corps as a firefighter but was later retrained as an Aviation Operations Specialist. My assignment was with the Operations Section at Marine Attack Training Squadron 203 (VMAT-203), Marine Corps Air Station Cherry Point, North Carolina. This was the squadron that trained Marine Corps aviators to fly the AV-8B Harrier. Since being assigned to the unit, I had been afforded many opportunities that appealed to my skills, abilities, and interests. One of those was related to military intelligence.

As a training squadron, VMAT-203 did not have an Intelligence section. Consequently, the instructor pilots were not always exposed to the same information as their counterparts in other squadrons. I was approached by my immediate supervisor, Gunnery Sergeant (Gunny) Rosemond, who told me Captain Wheeler wanted to speak with me. Wheeler, one of the instructor pilots, was aware of the problem and the negative impact on the other instructors in our unit. Furthermore, he had overheard me express similar concerns to Gunny Rosemond. Captain Wheeler asked if I was interested in working on the problem, and I readily accepted.

Arrangements were made for a temporary, month-long assignment at the Intelligence section of Marine Aircraft Group 32, across the street from our hangar. Captain Wheeler directed me to immerse myself as much as possible in the identification of aircraft, ships, artillery, and armor. He wanted me to apply that knowledge and help the instructor pilots of VMAT-203 remain current with enemy threats. I thoroughly enjoyed the assignment and the month went by more quickly then I wanted. Returning to my unit, I was loaded with slides, posters, information, and other materials the pilots used to help them stay proficient in identifying both friendly and enemy military equipment.

During my time in the military, I held a security clearance and I took the associated responsibilities seriously. The regulations and procedures governing the handling and dissemination of classified material were not my only guideposts. Something much deeper was involved, and that was integrity. Although Captain Wheeler never explicitly referred to my integrity, it was implied based on the trust he had in me to carry out the assignment.

A reputation of integrity brings rewards such as gaining the trust of your boss and others, working beyond your scope of responsibility, and peace of mind knowing you are doing the right thing. However, at times there may be a price to pay for maintaining integrity. This requires personal courage, determination, and intestinal fortitude. Unfortunately, I have sometimes been berated, shunned, and falsely accused because of doing right.

THE SURPRISES OF INTEGRITY

At times you may be assigned projects you did not ask for because your integrity built a foundation of trust with your boss.

During my time at MCAS Cherry Point, I often drove by an ominous-looking compound that resembled a prisoner-of-war camp. From my limited drive-by view, the fenced-in prison looked like some of the photos I had seen from the Vietnam era. There was a guard tower next to the road and a loudspeaker blared in a monotone voice, "You are now a prisoner of the People's Republic." This little slice of paradise was SERE school—an acronym for survival, evasion, resistance, and escape.

SERE school was a required training course for pilots and the enlisted aircrews. In order to supplement their teaching staff, the school sought volunteers to function as enemy troops to hunt and capture SERE students. Each month I volunteered for the assignment and each month I was turned down. The process had turned into a ritual for me. Imagine my excitement when Gunny Rosemond pulled me aside and said he had a special assignment for me. I thought, *Finally! I'm going to be an aggressor at SERE school.*

Gunny said I was being assigned extra duty with the SACO. What!? SACO!? I thought he was joking because SACO stands for the Substance Abuse Control Officer. Rosemond said that Sergeant Robinson and I would work for Captain Myers. The primary mission of our extra duty was conducting the "golden flow test"—in other words, we would supervise Marines urinating in plastic cups for random drug testing.

As the initial shock wore off, I asked, "But Gunny, why me?!" Apparently I thought my rank and status in life had endowed me as a special instrument of the Marine Corps, and I was above this type of humiliating duty. I will always remember what Gunny Rosemond said. "Sergeant Davis, it's because we trust you. We know you don't drink and you don't do drugs. We trust you and we need you to do it."

Gunny's comments were humbling. His words were genuine and sincere. They were also meaningful and complimentary. My unit wanted and needed someone with integrity who could be trusted to perform the job, and they chose me. Random testing was conducted several times a month. Robinson and I collected the disgusting samples and placed them in brown cardboard boxes. When the boxes were full, we sealed them with evidence tape, completed the associated paperwork, and transported the boxes to the base lab for further processing. Also, as part of our undesirable assignment, we too provided a sample each time to validate the integrity of the process.

Please do not allow the fear of unwanted or undesirable assignments to deter you from demonstrating integrity. However, should your integrity constantly land you in those positions, then it is time to talk with the boss. Be thankful for the trust bestowed upon you and the opportunities, but let your supervisor know how you feel. You should not be in a situation where you are the go-to person all the time. It's not good for you, your coworkers, your boss, or the organization.

THE PRICE AND PAIN OF INTEGRITY

When the Marine Corps changed my career field to Aviation Operations Specialist, I attended school at Naval Air Station Meridian, Mississippi. A small number of corporals and sergeants were attending various Marine Corps schools at the base, and periodically we were tasked as the Duty NCO (noncommissioned officer). We checked the barracks for security, ensured the junior Marines performing fire watch were awake, and patrolled areas of the base that commonly attracted Marines such as the Enlisted Club where alcohol was served. Simply put, the Duty NCO watched over the junior Marines to make sure there were no problems. If one did occur, we addressed the issue within the scope of our responsibility.

An important point of my next story is that we were Marines assigned to a U.S. Naval installation. Some may not be aware that the Marine Corps is part of the Department of the Navy. The Corps is an amphibious force and requires ships to get from Point A to Point B, hence a tremendous reliance on the Navy. The Navy supplies corpsmen (medics) to Marine combat units, along with medical and chaplain services at Marine installations. A healthy dose of rivalry also exists—some of it friendly, and some not so friendly.

I was the Duty NCO on a warm Friday night in November 1985. With the start of the weekend, I anticipated alcohol-fueled problems between Marines and sailors at the Enlisted Club. Later that evening, though, all was quiet. The only exceptions were two highly intoxicated individuals doubled up over toilets, driving the porcelain bus. As I returned to the small office in one of the barracks, I heard a loud commotion to my left. Suddenly I saw three Marines appear out of the dark, running past the barracks. Behind them, I heard the clop-clop-clop of shoes pounding on the pavement and a female voice yelling at the three Marines to stop. The person engaged in the pursuit was a Navy petty officer, and she was pregnant. Police officers refer to such information as clues. Something was clearly amiss. Joining in the foot pursuit, I yelled for my assistant to notify law enforcement, which the Navy refers to as the Master of Arms or MA. What had been a quiet night now involved an incident between the Navy and Marines.

Eventually the MA, the pregnant petty officer, and I caught the three Marines behind a dimly lit building. Immediately I recognized the three as Marines who had been in trouble more than once during the past month. There we were, standing in the dark with three young, healthy Marines who had just led a pregnant Navy petty officer on a foot chase. Why? They had been at the female barracks past the curfew time of 10 p.m. The petty officer had politely reminded Privates Bill, Bob, and Bud of the curfew and asked them to leave. Instead, the three chose to ignore her request. The petty officer then ordered them out of the area, but they decided to become insubordinate with her. I suspect the three Marines thought they could run off and the petty officer would drop the matter. They made the wrong assumption and the wrong choice.

The Navy MA asked what I wanted to do with them. I glanced at the petty officer, wondering if her baby suffered any harm from chasing the culprits. I was infuriated that three Marines put themselves in a position of forcing a pregnant woman to chase them. Regardless of interservice rivalries, Bill, Bob, and Bud demonstrated a lack of integrity, and disrespect toward the petty officer. They were unapologetic and wore a look of firm defiance on their faces. Everyone watched me, waiting for an answer. No doubt the privates assumed I would defend and protect them from the Navy because of the Marine Corps brotherhood. Would I take responsibility for the three Marines or turn them over to the MA?

Based on their troubled history and insubordination, and the petty officer's condition, I turned the three Marines over to the MA. They were taken into custody and transported to the brig (Navy and Marine Corps term for jail). I notified my immediate supervisor, Staff Sergeant Adams, about the incident. He went to the brig and arranged the release of Privates Bill, Bob, and Bud. Adams confined them to the barracks for the remainder of the weekend. They were only permitted to leave at mealtime, but under escort.

On Monday morning, the direct supervisor of the three offending Marines verbally dressed me down in front of the entire admin section. Staff Sergeant Furious berated me for getting the

Navy MA involved in the incident. He criticized me for shaming the Marine Corps and for not taking care of my brother Marines. My interpretation of his tirade was, *They are Marines, you are a Marine, and we never let the Navy do anything to us*—regardless of what happened, regardless of their insubordination, and regardless that they would put a pregnant female in a position to chase them. It probably goes without saying that I was utterly humiliated and dumbfounded by this man's reaction. Not only had these three Marines violated the Marine Corps leadership traits and principles, but Staff Sergeant Furious was defending them and demonstrating a lack of integrity on his part. Earlier in his career, he had served as a drill instructor and now he was treating me like a brand new recruit in boot camp. While he was in my face screaming, I started to question if I had made the right decision regarding the three Marines. I wondered whether or not it was just him, or were other NCOs the same way. Over the next few days, I became disheartened with the Marine Corps. My supervisors shunned me, but the other four NCOs in my class reaffirmed that I took the right actions.

Before the week ended, a disciplinary process was conducted by our commanding officer (CO). Besides myself, the individuals present were the CO, the sergeant major, the pregnant petty officer, the three offending Marines, my supervisor, and Staff Sergeant Furious. The CO was a lieutenant colonel, and after passing judgment on the three guilty Marines, he firmly dressed them down for their actions and behavior. I anxiously awaited my turn to be chewed out by the CO and then the sergeant major. Fortunately, neither felt the same way as Staff Sergeant Furious. It has been over thirty years since that incident and I cannot recall what punishment the three Marines received. However, I distinctly remember the CO telling the petty officer and myself that our actions and handling of the situation were correct. The look on the face of Staff Sergeant Furious was stunned disbelief. Afterward I never said anything to him and he never said anything to me, but I had an extreme sense of satisfaction. The commanding officer vindicated my actions.

Writing this story causes me to reflect on that evening in November 1985. Did I do the right thing by turning Privates Bill, Bud, and Bob over to the Navy MA and sending them to the brig? It has been thirty-four years since the incident occurred and if I were in that same situation today, I would handle it differently. But now I have the benefit of time, maturity, and years of experience under my belt. In 1985, my decision was based more on emotions than sound reasoning of leadership experience. Hindsight is almost always twenty-twenty, making past circumstances easier to interpret through a different lens. I could have accepted responsibility for the three Marines and confined them to the barracks, awaiting further direction from my supervisor. I did not compromise my integrity by turning them over to the MA, but neither would I have compromised my integrity by accepting responsibility for them.

In the end, the privates were wrong and they were held accountable for their choices and actions. I hope Bill, Bob and Bud learned from that experience and changed. I hope they learned a lesson about integrity and respect. I hope they successfully fulfilled their commitment to the Marine Corps, and I hope they have enjoyed a successful life since that time.

THE SATISFACTION OF INTEGRITY

After reading the previous two stories, you may question whether having and maintaining integrity is worth the trouble. Yes it is, because you and I must live with ourselves. At the end of my life I will stand before God and answer for my actions. That fact alone helps me make the right choices, but it does not necessarily ease the anguish that sometimes accompanies doing the right thing.

In the long run the pain and humiliation that come with being berated and shunned are worth it. The sense of frustration that comes with undesirable assignments is worth it. Maintaining our integrity builds courage, develops confidence, and reaps the reward of a clean and clear conscience. Are you not sure what to do? Then always choose to do right. Proverbs 11:3 states: "The integrity of the upright will guide them . . ."

Practical Application

- Integrity is the rock-solid foundation of leadership. Build your house of character on that premise.
- Enjoy the rewards that accompany integrity, such as challenging and desirable assignments.
- Do not be surprised when you receive undesirable assignments because of your reputation for integrity. Accept them as a compliment, but at the same time, speak up if a trend is created.
- Always do right, regardless of what may happen to you personally. Understand there are times when you will pay a price for integrity. In the end, you will be happy you did the right thing.
- Take time to reflect on your experiences. Learn from them, but don't agonize over them.
- Maintaining integrity builds courage and develops confidence, while setting an example for others to follow.

A Painful, Defining Experience

October 29, 1929, is known as "Black Thursday," the first day of the Great Depression that lasted until 1939. The stock market crash spread worldwide with no regard for race, color, creed, or ethnicity. Throughout the nation, the financial crisis thrust thousands of people out of work and into economic hard times. It was a time of uncertainty, anxiety, and desperation. People learned to exist on meager earnings and families subsisted on scraps of food. Within a couple of years, World War II followed closely behind the Great Depression.

As if those hardships were not enough, death visited the Davis family in November 1946 when the grandfather I never met died of a heart attack. My dad, Dick, was sixteen years old. With two years remaining before graduation, my dad quit high school and went to work supporting his mother and younger brother. On June 25, 1950, North Korea attacked South Korea, pushing the United States into another war. Desiring to follow his brother's footsteps, my dad tried to join the Marine Corps. Unfortunately, he was medically rejected due to a heart murmur, a result of childhood rheumatic fever. His next stop was the Navy, but they too turned him down for the same medical reason. Undeterred, he went to the Coast Guard. Of course the heart murmur was still there, but he begged the doctors to overlook the issue and allow him to join the military. His persistent efforts paid off, and Dad enlisted as a machinist's mate, working in the engine room of Coast Guard ships and operating small boats. Regrettably, he suffered a knee injury after falling down a ladder on board a ship in the North Atlantic. He was medically discharged and returned to civilian life after nearly four years in the military.

Following his time in the Coast Guard, my dad worked as a bank teller where he met his future wife Mary. Leaving the bank, he went to work operating printing presses and did that job for several years. Eventually he became the general manager for Messick Brothers Construction Company in Bridgeton, New Jersey. That would be his final job.

Dick Davis has been described as an honest, hardworking, good man by those who remember him. When I think of my dad, characteristics such as honesty and truthfulness come to mind. His work ethic was unequaled and he expected the same from my brother and me. My mom and dad had a special, loving marriage and I never heard him utter a word in anger toward her. I remember them spending time and talking with one another at the kitchen table. Dad opened doors for my mom and showered her with honor and respect. He also taught my brother and me to do the same. He was the protector and provider of the family. Eventually he obtained his high school diploma. After working all day long, he attended night school at Rutgers University, pursuing a college degree. He faithfully helped in our church by singing in the choir, serving as a deacon, and providing oversight for a construction project. He was also involved with an organization named SCOPE, helping underprivileged minorities in South Jersey.

Unfortunately, Dad was also a man with a multitude of medical problems, suffering his first heart attack in February 1966. As his health continued to decline, he was forced into permanent disability and could no longer work. Up to that time Dad was the sole provider for our family, a role subsequently falling upon my mom. When Dad went on permanent disability, she joined the ranks of hundreds of South Jersey residents working in the factory at Wheaton Glass to support us.

I remember the morning of March 9, 1972, as if it were yesterday. I was fourteen years old and in the eighth grade at Myron L. Powell School in Cedarville, New Jersey. It was a beautiful, sunny and clear day, and void of the haze typically found in New Jersey. Mom left for work and as my brother and I prepared for school, I noticed something different about my dad. He was full of energy and happier than I had seen him in quite some time. Dad planned on cleaning the house and the refrigerator that day.

I always ran home after school and March 9 was no different. No different until I opened the door of our house, announced my presence, and was met by silence. I stepped around the kitchen table and found Dad's lifeless body lying on the floor. Sometime during the afternoon, he had suffered his final and fatal heart attack. The refrigerator door was open, a mustard jar was by his hand, and several items were on the kitchen table—a clear indication that his last activity on earth was cleaning out the refrigerator.

My brother and I lost our father and my mother lost her husband of seventeen years. Life forever changed for our family on that bright, sunny afternoon. The day of his funeral was cold, cloudy, gloomy, and windy. I wondered if the weather was a portent of our future without Dad. I felt deep pain, anguish, loneliness, and fearful emptiness. We were not in a unique situation, as many before and after us experienced the same pain of losing a loved one. Yet in many respects, the circumstances following my dad's death defined my future path.

In the days following his passing, and sometimes years after, I heard about his integrity and character. My dad led by example and I had seen his character and integrity in action for myself. I will always remember him saying, "If you're gonna do a job, then do it right, or don't do it at all."

Life is full of choices, but we cannot choose the consequences. I could have chosen to be a victim and allowed my father's death to take me down a path of drug use, crime, bouncing from one job to another, or any of a thousand things. Even then God's hand protected me from choices that could have destroyed my life. The death of my father was an extremely painful experience, but also one that shaped me.

Our integrity and character are of the utmost importance and we must protect both. People cannot take either of them from us, but our actions can certainly bolster, tarnish, or destroy those important traits. I have made some pretty stupid mistakes in my life, and you'll read about a few of them later in the book. However, looking back with the benefit of time, age, and experience, I continue to learn and grow from them. My dad was a man of integrity and it is my desire to emulate that quality.

2 *Earning Trust Is Paramount to Leadership* **Trust and Credibility**

"Trust is the glue of life. It's the most essential ingredient in effective communication. It's the foundational principle that holds all relationships."

— Stephen Covey, Author and Educator

Within the past five years, a new business emerged in Loveland, Colorado, named Emily's Delights. The owner is an enterprising entrepreneur who bakes cake pops. Emily's business motto is: "Making taste buds happy one cake pop at a time." Her baked goods are moist and delicious, and my taste buds jump with delight when I eat them. Emily lives a life of integrity, and her commitment to quality baking earns a level of trust and credibility with customers. Furthermore, the high quality of her cake pops reinforces the validity of the business motto. Some may say I have a biased opinion because Emily is my daughter. Perhaps I am not impartial, but nevertheless, my wife and I are thrilled with her character-based approach to business. Emily possesses a triad of strength.

A TRIAD OF STRENGTH

Remember in the last chapter when I said integrity is the rock-solid foundation of leadership? Resting upon that base and joining together at the top to form a triad are trust and credibility. Of the latter two characteristics, which comes first, trust or credibility? Neither one comes first, because they coexist, grow, and develop in unison. Remove one or the other and the triad collapses.

You should also understand that lacking trust and credibility with others does not always indicate an absence of integrity. Several factors impact credibility, such as education, training, experience, and reputation. For example, you may have a college degree and fundamental training in your profession, but lack experience as a newer member of an organization. As you continue to work hard, display integrity, and gain experience, you become more credible. Consequently, you earn more trust from your boss and those you work with. Therefore integrity, trust, and credibility create the triad of strength.

A SIMULATED PLANE CRASH

The Northern Colorado Regional Airport rests within the boundaries of the City of Loveland, and accordingly, the Loveland Fire Rescue Authority provides aircraft rescue firefighting (ARFF) services. Among their many responsibilities, the Federal Aviation Administration (FAA) also provides oversight for ARFF fire trucks, equipment, and training. Every three years, the FAA requires an exercise and drill. In 2010, our exercise was based on the crash of a McDonnell Douglas MD-80 jetliner, a plane capable of seating between 130–172 passengers, depending on the model of aircraft.

These types of exercises always involve evaluators to critique various aspects of the drill, e.g., firefighting, law enforcement, medical, airport staff, interagency cooperation, etc. I was the incident commander (IC) for this drill and the gentleman assigned as my evaluator was someone I had never met before. I wanted to know what experience and training he possessed. The gentleman had served in the U.S. Army Rangers as a communications operator for four years, but had no command experience. As a fellow veteran I respected and admired him as an Army Ranger, but he had no credibility with me as someone who should evaluate the IC because he never performed in that role.

In contrast, my friend Bruce was a retired Marine Corps major. He has command experience and served as an instructor at the Marine Corps Amphibious Warfare School in Quantico, Virginia. I extended an invitation for him to accompany me during the drill and observe what we were doing. I also asked Bruce to critique my performance and provide feedback. Just as the Army Ranger was not a firefighter, neither was Bruce. However, Bruce's background, experience, and training lent a level of professional credibility that I needed in order to receive an accurate evaluation.

Following the drill, the exercise coordinators conducted an after-action review (AAR). The Ranger reported on my actions as the IC, but his comments were generalized and generic, and lacked substance because he *never* functioned as an incident commander. However, the feedback provided by Bruce assisted with my professional development as an IC. His observations were credible because of his command experience. My personality meshed with that of the Ranger and we had much in common from the standpoint of veterans. But I believe the individual responsible for the evaluators failed by not assigning the Ranger to assess a function more aligned with his background and skill level.

THE IMPORTANCE OF TRUST

As we build credibility, we earn trust. Removing society's criminal element from the equation, I believe most people want to be trusted and to trust others. In high-risk occupations such as firefighting, law enforcement, the military, and other professions where danger is present, a lack of trust raises suspicions. Does this person have my back? Will they be responsible for hurting or killing someone? Business owners want to hire people they can trust with the cash register. When you are standing in the security line at the airport, you want TSA agents to be trustworthy. At a restaurant, you hand your credit card to the wait staff and trust your bank account will not be hacked. Lying prone in the dentist chair, you trust your hygienist is competent when she has a sharp instrument in her hand. When your car breaks down on the Kansas Turnpike, you hope and pray the tow truck operator is trustworthy. Regardless of the profession or situation, earning trust is paramount in leadership.

DESTROYING TRUST

On the afternoon of October 17, 1989, thousands of people driving and riding on I-880 in California implicitly placed trust in the engineers and contractors who designed and built the freeway. The project was completed in 1957 and consisted of an elevated section called the Cypress Structure. Throughout the years, workers installed seismic upgrades to protect the freeway in the event of an earthquake. Suddenly the 7.1 Loma Prieta earthquake struck the San Francisco region, creating havoc and wreaking destruction on buildings, highways, and bridges. The earthquake caused the collapse of a 3,970-foot section of the Cypress Structure, killing forty-two people.[2] Thirty-eight years had passed between the start of construction in 1951 and the earthquake. In spite of the fact the highway stood the test of time, had been reinforced more than once, and was used by thousands of motorists each day, the Cypress Structure still collapsed under tremendous stress and strain from the strong earthquake.

Trust is very much like the I-880 scenario. Time and effort are necessary to build trust, and may be a part of your character for several years. Just as suddenly as the Loma Prieta earthquake struck California, your actions can shake and destroy the very foundations of trust.

Imagine you wake up to a beautiful Saturday morning in late May. The sun is shining, the grass is green, and the flowers are in full bloom. It's a nice morning to relax on the patio with a cup of coffee while reading the newspaper. Unfolding the paper, you take a bite from a doughnut and begin to read, and suddenly you start gagging. You yell out to no one in particular, "What is this!?" In bold letters, the headline of the *Town Liar* reads, "Dr. Joe Schmuckatelli Arrested in Parking Lot of Influenza General Hospital." Dr. Schmuckatelli has been your primary care physician for the past five years. You are incredulous and say, "This can't be! Joe is a well-known and respected physician." The article describes how Joe was the subject of a months-long investigation by local law enforcement and the DEA (Drug Enforcement Administration). Allegedly he was affiliated with the notorious drug cartel, We Sella You Dope. Joe was caught red-handed peddling narcotics from the trunk of his car. Wow! In reality, the good doctor adheres to the "Hippocritic" oath. Within a few short minutes, you no longer trust Joe and he has no credibility as a physician.

Although we can chuckle at Joe and the fictitious story, a sad fact remains: far too often similar stories play out in families, businesses, government, and churches. We must attach as much importance to building and protecting trust as we do with our integrity. One of the worst things you can hear is, "I do not trust you." On the other hand, one of the best things said is, "I trust you."

Do not violate the trust others have placed in you. Additionally, recognize opportunities to show your trust in subordinates. Allow them to address issues beyond their scope of responsibility and do not micromanage. When subordinates know you trust them, their confidence builds and morale increases. I address more about this later in the chapter.

RELATIONSHIPS AND TRUST

A key element involving trust is the relationships we build. I gained a greater understanding of that when I served as the leader of the Loveland Fire Department Hazardous Materials Team from 1997–2006. I not only built relationships internally, but externally with regional fire service partners, the Colorado State Patrol Hazmat Team, and individuals in health and environmental protection agencies. In April 2006, I turned over the helm of the Loveland Fire Hazmat Team and assumed the leadership of our wildland firefighting program. Once again, I was afforded an opportunity to form relationships and build trust with an entirely different aspect of the fire service. Building on the experiences learned while leading the Hazmat Team, I asked one of our firefighters, Ron Hill, to arrange meetings between us, Larimer County Emergency Services (LCES), the Colorado State Forest Service (CSFS), and the United States Forest Service (USFS). By that point, I knew a successful program can only occur through cooperative relationships—and relationships are built on trust.

In June 2010, the Cow Creek Fire burned through the terrain of Rocky Mountain National Park, with the potential to escape the park boundaries and burn toward the small town of Glen Haven. Preparing for that possibility, resources were requested from surrounding agencies, including Loveland, to provide fire trucks for structure protection in the threatened area. I was placed in charge of a small group of fire trucks and firefighters, and at approximately 6 p.m. on a Friday, we started toward Glen Haven, but we never made it. As our group reached the west side of Loveland, a wildland fire was reported in the Big Thompson Canyon, which is part of our jurisdiction. Based on the location of the new fire, we would drive by it on the way to Glen Haven. I thought the fire might be small enough for us to stop, quickly extinguish the flames, and continue toward our destination.

We exited an area of the canyon known as the Narrows and I saw the new fire actively burning upslope on the north side of Round Mountain. Additionally, I observed trees torching. Torching occurs when the main body of fire preheats the surrounding vegetation. It was obvious we would not just stop, put the fire out, and be on our merry way to Glen Haven. I radioed our small group that we were going to stop and engage the fire. Contacting our dispatch center, I told them what we had, what we were doing, and what additional resources we needed. I also asked them to notify the appropriate individuals at the Cow Creek Fire to tell them we would not be able to continue with our original assignment. (As a side note, the Cow Creek Fire never escaped the park boundaries, Glen Haven was spared, and because of the Round Mountain Fire, Loveland had no further involvement with the Cow Creek Fire.)

While our crews began fighting the fire, myself and another chief officer from Loveland Fire Rescue named Bill established an incident command structure. Over the next couple of hours, additional resources arrived. We also received information from a reconnaissance helicopter that structures were threatened and the fire was burning into steep terrain. Normally aircraft would have been available to attack the fire. However, due to the Cow Creek Fire and approaching sundown, these assets were not available. After sunset we made a decision to pull our firefighters off the line based on nightfall, steep terrain, and erratic fire behavior.

Another factor influencing our decision revolved around limited resource availability due to the Cow Creek Fire.

Earlier in the evening, when Bill and I mapped the location of the fire's origin, we determined it was burning on USFS land. Consequently, our command structure included their personnel. Little did I know that by Saturday afternoon the point of origin would turn into a point of contention between Loveland Fire, the USFS, and the Larimer County Sheriff's Office. As Friday evening wore on, we developed a plan for the next twenty-four hours. We decided Bill would remain on the fire overnight with the USFS incident commander and I would return in the morning.

MONEY FROM THE SKY

The next morning the USFS incident commander told me additional resources had been ordered overnight. The resources included two Type 1 hotshot crews and additional federal fire engines. Furthermore, two heavy air tankers, a SEAT (single-engine air tanker), and a large Sikorsky Skycrane helicopter had been ordered to help fight the fire. All appeared to be going well with the operation, and the threatened structures had resources assigned to them for protection. I spent the morning checking on firefighting personnel and watching the progression of the fire. I also watched the aerial display of the SEAT, heavy tankers, and helicopters dropping retardant and water to help the ground firefighting effort.

In the early afternoon we were notified of a thunderstorm approaching the area. These cells can be a portent of danger due to lightning, hail, high winds, sudden downdrafts, and wind shifts. Many of us remembered the South Mountain Fire near Glenwood Springs, Colorado. On July 6, 1994, a thunderstorm cell created erratic winds leading to the deaths of fourteen firefighters. We watched the approaching storm closely as the sky turned dark gray. Lightning began to bounce around us and supervisors ordered their personnel to take safety precautions. Suddenly, as if someone turned on a light, the clouds let loose with a true gully washer. Everyone on the fire line was drenched, and those of us who had vehicles were lucky enough to take refuge inside of them and wait out the storm. Once the storm passed, we saw a positive impact on the fire. There had been a wind shift, but the heavy rain extinguished the active fire front and slowed the forward progress of the flames.

All appeared to be well. That is, until the Larimer County undersheriff and the sergeant in charge of Larimer County Emergency Services approached me and said, "Hey Rick! Remember Senate Bill 20? Well . . . Loveland is going to have to pay for this fire."

I was dumbfounded. A couple of hours earlier, I had watched as heavy air tankers dropped red retardant along the fire line, but now I envisioned those same tankers depositing a wall of green one-hundred-dollar bills from the sky to incinerate in the flames.

The undersheriff and sergeant were referring to a Colorado Senate bill enacted in 2009, stating that until a delegation of authority was signed between the local jurisdiction and the county sheriff, the local agency would bear all of the financial costs of a wildland fire. Up to this point of the fire I had not considered a delegation of authority because the previous evening Bill and I had plotted the origin of the fire on USFS property. Therefore I assumed the Feds were responsible for all costs. The undersheriff and sergeant said the Feds were contending the point of origin and claimed it was on land owned by the City of Loveland. If that were true, then Bill and I had not only located the wrong point of origin, but Loveland was, in fact, financially responsible until a delegation of authority was signed.

I asked the undersheriff and the sergeant, "How much money?"

They both chuckled and said, "A lot of money," and began to rattle off a list. The hotshot crews were $5,000 per day, the heavy air tankers were $5,000 per drop, and the Sikorsky Skycrane was $25,000 a day. They didn't include the estimated costs of other resources on scene, but I heard enough to make my head spin. I generally avoid doing math in public because I will embarrass myself. However, I quickly calculated that we could easily reach a million dollars. My mind flooded with a thousand other thoughts, most negative. For those who don't work in emergency services, understand that Loveland Fire Rescue places tremendous responsibility on the shoulders of battalion chiefs. Everything from running daily operations at the shift level to leading personnel. Even greater is the trust placed in us to ensure the safety and well-being of our firefighters during emergencies. I started imagining the worst outcomes. Did I destroy the trust placed in me by the organization? What other consequences would arise from the Round Mountain Fire?

THE MEETING

A decision was made that the undersheriff, the sergeant, and I would meet with the USFS Fire Management Officer (FMO) of the Canyon Lakes Ranger District to discuss what agency was financially responsible. I felt good about that because I knew the FMO and he lived in my neighborhood. However, I was uneasy about having to notify the fire chief, Randy Mirowski, of what was taking place. Because of our location, cell phone service was nonexistent and I could not call the fire chief. I had our dispatch center notify the chief and our conversation took place via the not-so-private radio.

I took a breath and told him that Loveland Fire might be responsible for a lot of money. I informed him about the meeting with the FMO and Sheriff's Office, and said they wanted a representative from Loveland Fire to be present. Based on our potential for financial responsibility, I assumed the fire chief would go to the meeting. Much to my surprise, Chief Mirowski said he trusted me to represent Loveland and knew I could handle the negotiations between the other two agencies.

Before the sun went down on Saturday, a delegation of authority was signed detailing what agency was responsible for the various aspects of the Round Mountain Fire. However, the issue of who would pay for the resources assigned to the fire still loomed on the horizon and was not settled that night. Fortunately, after several post-fire meetings, Loveland was not financially responsible for the fire. In the end the USFS confirmed that Bill and I were correct, the fire originated on USFS land and the Feds were responsible for the costs.

What unfolded that Saturday afternoon was a display of trust the fire chief had with me and my abilities to address the financial issues. I am fully aware there are fire chiefs in this country who would have driven to the meeting to negotiate with the other parties. Frankly, if Chief Mirowski had said he was going to attend the meeting, I would not have thought anything about it. After all, as the fire chief, he had overall responsibility. But he did not do that. He voiced his trust in me and he had confidence I would handle the matter at hand. That was a tremendous morale and confidence booster.

When you are responsible for others who report to you, recognize those opportunities to show your trust in them, as it will pay off in high dividends. Also, work hard at building and maintaining your trust with others, as that too will pay off in the end.

Practical Application

- Integrity, credibility, and trust form a triad of strength.
- Trust and credibility work hand-in-hand to create a synergistic effect. In other words, they feed off of one another.
- Credibility and trust are based on many factors including education, training, and experience.
- Regardless of your profession or career path, trust is important. Our employers, subordinates, families, and friends want trusted leaders.
- Don't destroy the trust and credibility you have worked hard to earn. Writing in I Timothy 6:20 the Apostle Paul said, "O Timothy! Guard what was committed to your trust . . ."
- We saw in the previous chapter that integrity leads to greater responsibilities. The same occurs with trust and credibility.
- When leaders recognize a subordinate's credibility and the leader places trust in that person, the positive impact on morale and confidence-building are exponential for all parties involved.

A Boyhood Dream

Integrity, trust, and credibility are not magically bestowed upon a person overnight. A considerable amount of time has been involved for my daughter Emily to learn baking skills. Likewise, time is involved in earning trust and credibility. And time requires patience, a quality many people struggle with. Today's society expects instant gratification. We are besieged with fast-food restaurants, microwave meals, and power drinks. We access the information highway from our phones and read about the latest world tragedies moments after they occur. We want everything right now, including trust. However, life does not work that way. We must patiently wait for the rewards that follow the consistent and persistent development of trust and credibility.

Following my dad's death in 1972, my interest in becoming a firefighter spiked. But there were obstacles to overcome. One problem was the fact that Cedarville, New Jersey, is a small town with a volunteer fire department. Therefore, the only guarantee of finding someone at the firehouse was during training or meeting nights, or when there was a fire. Another obstacle was my shyness. I was so quiet around people it was necessary to check my pulse to see if I was still alive.

I was fourteen years old and in the eighth grade. Walking to and from school, I passed the firehouse and dreamed of being inside the building amongst the shiny fire engines. Often I would stop and stare through the glass, wondering what it would be like as a firefighter. During that period, a large red siren mounted on a tower alerted firefighters and townspeople of a fire. Ever since I was a little boy I had run to the street in front of our house when the siren blew, hoping to see the trucks pull out of the station, and better yet, drive by the house! One summer afternoon in 1972 when the siren sounded, a tremendous urge flowed over me like a wave. I *had* to go to the firehouse to see what was happening. I remember being gripped with the fear of uncertainty. Would anyone be there? Did they all go to the fire? If someone was there, would they tell me to get lost? A hundred other questions ran through my mind as well. In the end the compelling desire to see inside the firehouse and find out what was going on was a tsunami overcoming any fears associated with being shy.

I walked approximately two hundred yards to the Cedarville Fire Company Number 1, unsure of what or who would greet me. By then all the trucks had left the firehouse and one person remained. His name was Art French, known throughout town as Frenchie. Everyone knew Frenchie. He and my Aunt Phyllis worked for Danzenbaker's International Farmall adjacent to the firehouse. Frenchie knew of my interest in firefighting and would send fire equipment catalogs home with Aunt Phyllis to pass on to me. Before I was even in grade school, Frenchie had arranged opportunities for my dad to take me to the firehouse. The firefighters had lifted me into the cab of the trucks and I can only imagine the smile on my face. Frenchie was also instrumental in my ability to ride on the town's newest fire engine in the 1961 Memorial Day parade. That afternoon in 1972, Frenchie welcomed me with open arms into the mesmerizing world of the firehouse.

From that day forward there was no looking back. Whenever I was home and there was a fire, I ran to the firehouse. Eventually I would get out of bed in the middle of the night to see what was going on when the siren sounded. My mom later shared with me that people couldn't believe she allowed me to go there at night. She told them I wanted to be a firefighter, and at least she knew where I was. At the firehouse I always watched quietly and listened to what took place around me. Ultimately I went to the firehouse on training nights, again watching and listening.

Frenchie had reached the point where he was no longer actively fighting fires, but he was the most loyal and faithful firefighter I knew at the time. When an alarm was received, Frenchie went to the firehouse, wrote the address on a chalkboard, and operated the base station radio. If help was needed at the scene of the emergency, Frenchie was the person who summoned the needed resources. He was an integral member of the fire department.

One afternoon when I was approximately sixteen, I was at the firehouse with Frenchie, sweeping the floors, when the phone rang. Frenchie said, “Grab the phone, Rick.” That may not sound like much, but to a sixteen-year-old kid who wanted to be a firefighter, it was huge. Frenchie trusted me to answer the firehouse phone! Wow! Not long after that, I graduated to speaking on the radio with the firefighters on the scene of an incident. I developed trust and credibility not only with Frenchie, but also with the fire chief, Mike Scarlato, and other members of the department. The rewards came in the form of being trusted to call other fire departments when help was needed in Cedarville.

The ultimate prize was becoming a member of the Cedarville Fire Company Number 1 when I turned eighteen.

Over the years, I have been rewarded with many unique and challenging opportunities because of integrity, trust, credibility, and character. Trust is earned and credibility is developed over time. Work hard on both and protect them. I guarantee you will see a lifetime of rewards for the effort.

3 *It's Alive!* Inheriting an Organizational Monster

"The way out of trouble is never as simple as the way in."

— Edgar Watson Howe, Novelist and Editor

I enjoy watching many of the old black-and-white classic Hollywood films. One of those is the 1931 Universal Studios production of *Frankenstein.* The monster was played by actor Boris Karloff. Colin Clive portrayed Dr. Frankenstein; his facial expressions and crazed eyes depicted a deeply disturbed individual. The good doctor had invited three guests into his foreboding laboratory to observe an experiment intended to create a new life. His hunchbacked assistant, Igor, hovered sinisterly nearby. Frankenstein moved to a table and pulled back a sheet revealing a hideous-looking creature sewn together from body parts stolen from graveyards. Outside, lightning flashed in a raging thunderstorm. When Frankenstein pushed the levers of his equipment, electricity began to pulse and sizzle between metal spheres. Frankenstein raised the table to an opening in the roof to take advantage of the intense electrical storm. Lowering the table to the floor, he watched as the monster began to move and lift a hand. Frankenstein softly muttered in an evil tone, "It's alive!" Eventually his voice rose to a crescendo repeating, "It's alive!"

What I just described is pure fiction, but unfortunately monsters exist in many organizations. All too often they are created and fed by the very people who employ them. Imagine you have finally been promoted after years of hard work and effort. Breathing a sigh of relief that you made it, you bask in the news about the accompanying pay raise. Although you may be slightly apprehensive about the new responsibilities, you still look forward to the challenge. Then the boss drops the bombshell. You just inherited your organization's Frankenstein. Oh no!

WHO ARE THESE MONSTERS?

In Matthew 7:15 Jesus said, "Beware of false prophets, who come to you in sheep's clothing, but inwardly they are ravenous wolves." This is an accurate description of organizational monsters. They are smooth-talking, suave individuals who know how to provide the right answers, often appealing to those who are easily deceived. Their inner character is often masked by an outgoing personality. They are the individuals who were hired for some unknown, odd reason. Many times, they look good on paper and their resumé appears to have been written by Shakespeare himself. During the interview, "Dr. Jekyll" holds the audience captive with tales of incredible feats accomplished at previous jobs. Mouths gape open wide and some wipe a tear of joy from the side of their eye, silently proclaiming, "Finally! We have the opportunity to hire St. Augustine!" The members of the interview panel slap each other on the back, congratulating one another for a job well done. They have finally found the person who most likely can not only cure cancer, but bring peace to the Middle East as well. They triumphantly stride into the boss's office and make a glowing, emphatic recommendation that this person be hired immediately. To do anything less would surely bring the institution to the brink of failure.

When the announcement is made that Dr. Jekyll has been hired, those familiar with this person are amazed and dumbfounded at how this possibly could have happened. Now it is their mouths that have dropped to the floor, but not because of the amazing achievements of Dr. Jekyll. It is because they cannot believe a group of supposedly intelligent people sitting on a hiring panel would be that duped into recommending this person for employment. They wonder why there is not a requirement for mandatory drug and alcohol screening in order to be a member of such a panel.

Meanwhile, on the other side of town at Jekyll's previous employer, they are throwing one of the wildest parties known to mankind because he's gone. To an outsider, their joy and revelry look like the celebrations at the end of World War II.

THE EVIL CHANGE

As time progresses, Dr. Jekyll begins to display characteristics and tendencies that are less endearing to others; however, to those who hired him he still appears to be a saint. Let no one be fooled, as Dr. Jekyll knows how to play the game. He knows what it takes to stay employed and he knows there is a probation period that he must successfully complete in order to keep his job.

The magical day arrives: the end of probation. Shortly afterward Jekyll rubs his hands together and his eyebrows scrunch in toward his devilish nose. He looks slyly upward and mutters in a deep, menacing tone, "Moo-ha-ha, I've made it! I'm no longer an at-will employee. They can only get rid of me for cause!" Lightning flashes! Thunder crashes and another organizational monster has been created.

The clever Dr. Jekyll has transformed into Mr. Hyde, all the while continuing on his devious, scheming paths. Every day his persona changes, depending on who he interacts with. If he speaks with someone who helps his career, then he is Dr. Jekyll. If he arrogantly believes the interface is with someone of lesser stature, he turns into Mr. Hyde. The pattern continues for several years. Eventually he is promoted into a supervisory position.

The employees who have worked with this individual are astonished at what they believe to be incredible depths of stupidity. They not only ask why he was hired in the first place, but they wonder why he was promoted. The employee rumor mill now spins at full speed. There is rampant speculation that Jekyll bribed the person who promoted him. Others are convinced that Jekyll possesses scandalous information on key figures and his promotion must be a case of extortion. Listening to the various theories flying around the room, you shake your head in disgust and walk off. Your confidence in the so-called leadership of the organization is rapidly eroding. You and Jekyll have become supervisory peers. As much as you can't stomach the thought of his promotion, you mutter, "Well, he may be a peer, but thank God he doesn't work for me."

THE MUCH-AWAITED PROMOTION

A couple of years pass and much to your chagrin, you and Jekyll are now competing for the next level of supervision. Since becoming peers you have watched the amazing transformation between Dr. Jekyll and Mr. Hyde play out time after time. One moment he is kissing the boss's rear end, and ten minutes later he intimidates an employee. You try to fight off the thoughts, but you can't help but wonder if bribery or extortion will come into play again. Looking across the room at Jekyll you ask yourself, "Are they *that* stupid to promote him again!?" Determined to do your best, you press forward and dismiss any thoughts of Jekyll.

When your boss calls you into the office, she shakes your hand and congratulates you on the new promotion. Without skipping a beat she says, "Oh by the way, Dr. Jekyll will be working for you and there will be no divorce between the two of you. It boils down to who goes first." In a matter of moments, Dr. Jekyll and Mr. Hyde have become *your* problem.

Although it is of little consolation, these are the types of situations creating job security for the psychologists, counselors, and human behavior researchers of the world. So what are you going to do? You had absolutely no say in the hiring or promotion of this person. Not only that, but in spite of Jekyll and Hyde's unbelievable behavior and poor job performance, his supervisors repeatedly showered him with glowing performance reviews and evaluations. And what is more incredible, those reviews were written by people who used a string of adjectives and expletives whenever they spoke about him behind closed doors.

Preposterous! Amazing! Astounding! But this scenario happens all the time in the workplace.

WHY THE MONSTERS ARE CREATED

Before continuing, please understand I am not writing about the loyal, trustworthy, and dependable employee who needs coaching to overcome a problem or requires an occasional course correction. Be perfectly clear that I am referring to the organization's bad apple who you inherited. The person requiring progressive discipline. And please note I am not talking about a witch hunt. Any action taken with an employee must be moral, ethical, and legal. Admittedly, it is difficult to enter a situation such as this and not be jaded by emotions about the swift, tactical options you want to take. Deep down you would love to call in an airstrike. But this is where integrity comes into play: do what is right.

Why do supervisors turn a blind eye to these types of people? Why is this type of behavior allowed to continue? Why weren't the performance issues dealt with before? Because of supervisory fear! Fear I won't be liked. Fear I can't be friends with this person. Fear he will rally allies to his side and make me look bad. Fear he won't do what I say. Fear of confrontation. Fear he is friends with another supervisor and that person will come after me. Fear I will be viewed as violating an unwritten code of protection. Fear I won't be part of the brotherhood or sisterhood because I handled the problem. Fear he might file a grievance against me. Fear he might get a lawyer. And the list of fears goes on and on. The Bible sums it up quite well in Proverbs 29:25, "The fear of man brings a snare, But whoever trusts in the Lord shall be safe."

These scenarios are unfortunate, sad, and disgusting, but I have seen them play out far too many times over the years. The fear of one or more people has ensnared and imprisoned supervisors and so-called leadership of organizations. Let's not mince words. If you have fallen into this trap then you are no longer the leader; you have become the manipulated and controlled. And make no mistake about it, more people in our organizations see what is going on than we may ever realize. Not only that, but they are talking about it behind the leader's back. Employees who are doing a good job ask, "Why aren't they doing something about it?" Supervisors falling into this category are similar to farmers sowing the seeds of discontent. The harvest is frustrated employees not trusting the leadership of the organization. Morale *will* suffer and cynicism *will* become the new standard.

Apathy is another reason why problem employees are not addressed. Previous supervisors may have said, "Why should I deal with the problem? It doesn't matter what happens because nothing will change." It could be the supervisor was nearing the end of their career and did not want to deal with the personnel headache at a late stage in the game. That person may think, "Why should I be the one to do anything now? I'm out of here in less than a year and I don't want to rock the boat." These are only a few explanations for why someone has not dealt with the issue, but they are lame excuses. Many years ago, my wife heard someone say that an excuse is the skin of reason stuffed with a lie. It is good to remember that an excuse is a failure on the part of an individual to accept responsibility for their actions and behavior.

TAKING ACTION

Now that we have discussed a sampling of the many reasons why problem employees are not dealt with, let's turn to what you need to do as a supervisor. Jekyll is now working for you and the boss said there will be no divorce in this situation. It is your responsibility to pick up the pieces and begin to right the wrongs of the past. As you consider your options, never lose sight of the fact that employee problems like this never go away on their own. Consider this: If you are diagnosed with cancer, would you seek treatment or wait for the disease to get better and go away by itself? Unless you are some kind of lunatic, you will go to the doctor and take the necessary steps to rid your body of the cancer that is destroying you. Yes, dealing with personnel problems is much easier said than done. And rest assured they involve a lot of hard work and a considerable amount of time.

Before discussing the topic of discipline, something must be accomplished on your part as the supervisor. When you start working with Dr. Jekyll, ensure he understands both the organizational expectations and yours. However, do not establish unrealistic or unachievable expectations for the other person. I have witnessed this over the years and it only serves to create more frustration on the part of everyone involved. Treat the individual with respect, listen to what they are saying, and do not interrupt. Also, ask Dr. Jekyll what he wants to accomplish in life, including at work. This might be the first time someone has actually asked him that question. Respect goes a long way with people, and your organizational monster may think, "Hey, for once I have a supervisor who's serious about things, but also one who cares." This does not make you a pushover or a weakling. You are demonstrating leadership.

This is also the time to let Jekyll and Hyde know you will hold him accountable for his performance, actions, and behavior. It is possible you are the first true leader this person has worked for in years. Jekyll may be the type of person who respects leadership but disdains weak people trying to manage him. There is a possibility his past supervisors did not have any leadership training and they had no idea how to address the behavior with Jekyll. Conceivably, his past supervisors may have been more interested in preserving their reputations and deliberately overlooked Jekyll's monstrous tendencies. They further contributed to the problem by cowardly writing glowing performance evaluations.

Anytime you are engaged in a coaching and counseling session, or involved in a progressive disciplinary process, make sure you have a method of keeping notes. You may use a small pad of paper, a Word document, an electronic device, or even send yourself an email. Regardless of the method that works best, you need to track what is being said, because our memories can and will fail us. When dealing with behavior and performance problems, we need to provide specific examples. Generalities based on memory do not serve a useful purpose and are often counterproductive. Citing specific examples creates an atmosphere to properly address problems and sets the tone to move forward. True leaders desire to see positive changes in the lives of others and it starts by providing examples.

PEOPLE CAN CHANGE

In my experience, the people who truly change are unfortunately in the minority. However, leaders realize that people can and do change. Oftentimes this is brought about by being firm with the other person. Not threatening or intimidating, but resolute with the actions that must take place to correct the problem. This may have been absent with other supervisors in Jekyll's past.

As a good leader, you are now the one applying the needed pressure to bring about the desired change.

Warning! If you believe people never change, then you will constantly be at war or in retreat with the problem employees. The notion that people do not change is a cynical mindset to avoid. Furthermore, that line of thinking nullifies the transforming work of Christ. A prime example of change is the Apostle Paul, who went from terrorizing, tormenting, and imprisoning Christians to one of the boldest preachers known to mankind. One only needs to read the story about Saul of Tarsus in Acts Chapter 9 of the Bible to learn about people changing. In Verse 5, Jesus said, "I am Jesus, whom you are persecuting. It is hard for you to kick against the goads." From that point forward, Paul's life forever changed.

Believing that people never change is another way of devaluing others. I know when I am not valued or respected, and so do you. As a leader, if you adhere to the following analogy, it is time to evaluate why. I'm speaking of a fist and a bucket of water. A supervisor tells an employee to thrust a fist into a bucket of water up to the elbow, and then remove it. Once they remove it, of course, the void is filled by the water. The supervisor says, "See! There's no hole left in the water because it was replaced and we can replace you too, just like that!" This misguided example downplays a person's role and importance within the organization. Even if they are causing trouble, leaders should not use this example, because it only creates greater problems. If you are fond of using the fist and bucket analogy, you are revealing what you truly think of people: worthless and replaceable.

Fortunately, God does not believe this. Psalm 139:14 states, "I will praise You, for I am fearfully and wonderfully made; Marvelous are Your works, and that my soul knows very well." A human being that is wonderfully and fearfully made by God has value. Yes, personnel problems create angst and frustration in your life and at times you will probably want to scream at the top of your lungs. Avoid slipping into a frame of mind devaluing the other individual. If that occurs, you will be caught in a downward spiral with unwanted outcomes. With that being said, the fact remains that some people will choose not to change. Later in the chapter,

I discuss how to deal with those individuals regarding accurate documentation.

THE VAMPIRE

Another monster is the vampire. They sink their sharp fangs into the neck of a leader and suck the lifeblood out of you and others. In Bram Stoker's story of Count Dracula, several methods were employed to fend off the vampire, including exposure to light, garlic, and a silver stake. If and when you deal with Vladovitch the Vampire, drag him into the light of integrity. Hang the garlic cloves of courage around your neck, and use the silver stake of organizational rules, regulations, and policies. If and when Vladovitch threatens to report you to the Human Resources Department or go to a lawyer, then remain firm and resolute, continue to do your job, and do not give in to his intimidation tactics.

Several years ago, I had a vampire on my shift who was sucking the life out of me and others. After my promotion to battalion chief, I inherited an individual who created immense problems for both the organization and himself. Additionally, no one wanted to work with this guy. At first I thought that surely my great leadership skills would have a positive impact on his life. After all, Vladovitch might give up his blood-sucking tendencies and change for the better. I envisioned him going through the remainder of his career as a liked and productive individual, similar to the transformation experienced by Ebenezer Scrooge after three ghosts visited him on Christmas Eve. Well, that was not the case, and I spent hours dealing with this person.

I knew the stress of the situation was taking an emotional and physical toll on my life, but I had no idea what it was doing to others—until one afternoon when I visited the fire station where Vladovitch the Vampire worked. He had called in sick that day so I knew the visit would be more pleasant than normal. When I was getting ready to leave the station, one of the Vampire's firefighters asked to speak with me alone. He said, "Chief, when I speak to others on the shift, they tell me about your station visits and the time you spend with them. You pass on information, you mentor them, you tell them war stories about your career, and you laugh with them. Why don't you do that with me? When you visit the station, you say hello then you take my lieutenant into another room and close the door. You're in there for a long time and when you come out you tell me goodbye and leave. Why don't you spend time with me like you do with others on the shift?"

I can still hear his words ringing in my mind as if they were spoken ten minutes ago. I stood there looking at him with a sharp pain in my stomach as if I had been punched by the boxer George Foreman. This man had the courage to confront me with his concern, and he was right on target. I came to the stark realization that I was allowing Vladovitch the Vampire to consume so much of my time that I was neglecting the needs and desires of the firefighter speaking to me. The firefighter was not causing any problems, and he desired to learn from my experiences and be mentored. Although he was aware of organizational information, the firefighter wanted an opportunity to ask questions in order to gain greater clarity on department issues and concerns. In short, he wanted me to spend time with him like I did with the crews in the other stations. I had allowed the blood-sucking actions of Vladovitch the Vampire to hinder my ability to properly lead the firefighter I was speaking with. I apologized to the firefighter, asked him to forgive me, and vowed I would never again allow someone to suck the life out of me.

We must know when to draw the line with people. In Proverbs 4:7 Solomon wrote, "Wisdom is the principal thing; Therefore get wisdom. And in all your getting, get understanding." Wisdom and understanding come about through experiences, and sometimes they are hard lessons to learn. Devoting too much time to a vampire leads to neglecting others. However, turning a blind eye to the vampire and concentrating on the easy parts of life only allow the monster to grow.

Unfortunately there are no black-and-white answers to the question of where to draw that line. This is only one of many reasons why we cannot practice the art of leadership in a vacuum. To learn we must seek help from other people and turn to good sources of information, such as books, articles, and more.

IMPORTANCE OF ACCURATE DOCUMENTATION

The story of Vladovitch the Vampire is sad. I realized that in spite of all the time spent with him, he continually resisted any and all efforts directed at change. I did not like the way he treated his crew. I did not like the way he attempted to manipulate, cajole, and control others. He was a constant energy drain on his subordinates, on his peers, on the department, and on me. I fought an uphill battle with this guy because his past supervisors had written glowing performance evaluations on him—all the while knowing who and what he was. They failed Vladovitch, the members of the department, and the citizens. A year later the Vampire left the department.

As a new supervisor, it is possible you have been given the authority to terminate someone if you believe that is what needs to be done. Frankly, that may be necessary to rid your organization of the hideous monsters lurking behind the walls. On the other hand, you may not have that kind of authority, and it will be necessary to work through a progressive disciplinary process. Which, I will add, is much more difficult if previous supervisors have always written good performance reports on the individual in question.

Why? Because the Human Resources Department will review the past evaluations and tell you this person cannot be fired because there is no previous documentation to support your recommendation. I experienced this very thing with Vladovitch the Vampire. I did not know who I was more angry with—previous supervisors who turned their heads and did nothing to correct the problem, or Vladovitch himself. Those other supervisors had been complacent and they contributed to his unacceptable behavior by not addressing the problem.

As leaders, we have an obligation to provide accurate documentation. We owe it to our subordinates, their peers, the organization, and to the people who will supervise them in the future. We also need to dismiss the thought of documentation always being used for correction and discipline. The majority of people assigned to me over the years have been motivated, hard-working, dedicated employees. Good behavior, excellent work performance, and positive attitudes need to be documented as well.

If you do become involved in a progressive disciplinary process with an employee, realize that you won't be the Lone Ranger trying to sift through everything required. There are bosses above you, the Human Resources and Legal departments, and possibly union representation for the employee in question. How performance and behavior issues are ultimately resolved depends a lot on what kind of support you receive from the top. Remember, some of the people in the chain of command may be responsible for hiring and promoting the organizational monster, and for writing their glowing reviews. If that is the case, it may be more difficult to deal with the problem at hand, but you still have an ethical obligation to do what is right. The circumstances involving the behavior of your superiors are beyond your oversight, but you do have control over your integrity. To do anything less equates to a failure to perform your duties. On the other hand, your boss may have replaced those poor supervisors, and that individual is just as anxious as you to bring the matter to a successful conclusion.

POSITIVE CHANGE

Earlier I wrote that people can and do change. Regardless of the leader's actions, the responsibility for making the right choice to change rests squarely on the shoulders of the employee. Will they resist, will they comply to save their position, or will they genuinely transform? We cannot begin to answer those questions until the leader courageously confronts the person and holds them accountable for their actions.

Far too many supervisors take the easy, groomed path to avoid the hard work. Do not make that choice! Grab a machete and start blazing a trail through the employee's tangled jungle of obstinate behavior, defiance, poor performance, and pride. Many times you will reach the other side of the jungle and discover that the employee did not survive the trip. On the other hand, you may hack your way through the jungle growth along the Nile River, emerging on the other side, and proclaiming as Henry Stanley did when he asked, "Dr. Livingstone, I presume?" You will experience a tremendous amount of satisfaction and happiness with the victory accompanying the changed life of your employee.

During my time in the Marine Corps, one of our junior Marines began to exhibit behavior and performance problems. The number of mistakes Lucy made increased, she became sluggish and lethargic, and she displayed an overall attitude of apathy. Compounding the issue was a sudden surge in the number of times Lucy reported to sick call. The matter came to a head one day when the Gunny (my boss) and I discussed concerns over her rapid decline. Once again, Lucy had notified us that she was going to sick call. Growing suspicious over her truthfulness, the Gunny told me to call the hospital and ask if Lucy was there. The Navy corpsman who answered the phone indicated that no one by her name had checked in. He said I should call the OB/GYN clinic, because many times female Marines went there instead of the main hospital. However, when I checked with that clinic the answer was the same: she had never been there.

Around noon, Lucy reported to work displaying signs of an obvious hangover. Red-faced, sluggish, and an overall attitude of "who cares?" We went to another room and I asked how she was doing and was everything alright. Lucy told me the doctor said she was dehydrated. She added a few other symptoms, attempting to validate her story. I asked how she was doing a second time and the story slightly changed. When I asked her the third time, she broke down crying and said, "You know, don't you?"

I told her I had called the hospital and OB/GYN clinic, and found out she had never reported to sick call. Lucy's absence and lying were a big deal in the military because she was considered UA (unauthorized absence). That is a punishable offense under the Uniform Code of Military Justice (UCMJ). Lucy told me she had recently started to drink heavily and lived in fear that we would find out. She expressed concern about becoming an alcoholic and needed help.

I thanked Lucy for admitting the truth and said we would get her assistance through the proper sources. I also said she would be held accountable for her behavior and actions. Although I possessed the authority to punish her with the weight of the UCMJ, I opted for a different route. Previously I described an incident at Naval Air Station Meridian, Mississippi, where I sent three Marines to the brig. During the time between that and this instance, I gained more experience as a leader and learned that the severe method is not always the most appropriate. Lucy's punishment was extra duty. Instead of performing her normal job, Lucy was ordered to field day the office spaces.

The grade school connotation of a field day indicates playing games outdoors. Not in the Marine Corps. A USMC field day means everything imaginable is thoroughly cleaned from top to bottom, side to side, inside-out, and outside-in. The following Saturday, she reported for work at 7 a.m. and was not finished until after 6 p.m. Before Lucy was allowed to go home, her work was inspected by an on-duty staff sergeant. Some may believe the punishment was harsh. Compared to the discipline she could have received, spending the day cleaning three offices was minor.

The initial meeting with her and the Saturday field day served as a wake-up call for Lucy and produced long-term, positive results. She checked into an alcohol rehab program, her life turned around, and Lucy returned to the productive individual we knew her to be. Lucy had been on the brink of turning into an organizational monster, but the outcome was encouraging and constructive. Why? Because Lucy was held accountable and she took responsibility for her life.

As a supervisor, there is a good chance you will be involved in situations similar to the ones described in this chapter. Granted, unless you're in the military, the field day option won't be available in your leadership toolbox. However, your toolbox should include the courage to confront, the courage to hold people accountable, and the courage to stay the course with them.

Practical Application

- Denying the existence of organizational monsters allows them to grow and thrive.
- Unattended monsters pull other people down, destroy morale, and erode confidence in the leadership of the organization.
- Monsters thrive with other monsters. Isolate them and do not allow your organization to become the latest box office horror thriller.
- Be courageous, confront the monsters, and hold them accountable.
- Document the good, the bad, and the ugly.
- Don't forget that you are not operating in a vacuum. Seek out and use the resources available to you for assistance.
- Remember that people can and do change. Your courageous action may serve as the catalyst for transformation in someone's life.

Court Jesters

On the opposite end of the scale from organizational monsters are the court jesters—people who do stupid things while attempting to draw attention to themselves. Some are socially awkward and believe their crazy antics will gain acceptance from the crowd they long to be part of. Others cross the line into the realm of becoming the village idiot. One example of the latter comes from my high school years in Bridgeton, New Jersey, when I was part of a graphic arts program during my junior and senior years. Mr. Blake was the teacher, and he taught me how to operate a Multilith 1250 offset printing press.

Blank paper was stacked at one end of the machine and adjustments could be made to accommodate the correct size and weight of the paper. A flexible, metal plate was positioned on one of the rotating drums and wiped with a liquid solution. As the press ran, ink adhered to raised letters and images on the plate. The paper passed between the drum with the plate and the impression drum. The paper was then grabbed by metal fingers attached to a chain-driven device. Completing the cycle, the finished product was delivered to a receiving tray.

The Multilith 1250 was a great printing press and I loved operating the machine. We printed letterhead, forms, tickets, and other documents for use in the high school. I experienced great satisfaction with the finished products. As a senior I had the unique opportunity to teach a student named Luther how to run the printing press. Luther was a nice guy and he is not a figment of my imagination, nor is he part of a made-up story. He was twenty-two years old and had returned to school once again to try and graduate. Although I don't believe he was successful, I'll give him credit for trying.

Luther was also a curious individual in his own funny, scientific way. As I increased the speed of the printing press, he paid close attention to everything I said and did. The machine was running smoothly and all was in working order. Suddenly the press stopped! Instead of listening to the sounds of air, paper, rotating drums, and gears operating in concert with one another, all I heard was the hum of the straining and burning electric motor on the press. Quickly turning off the power to the machine, I said, "What happened!?" While attempting to troubleshoot the problem, I looked at Luther, who had a blank stare on his face. Initially it was the type of blank stare that indicated I should know how to fix this thing. Then I found the source of the problem. A big, flathead screwdriver was wedged between the two drums—the same screwdriver that had been in Luther's hand when we started the job.

In my best South Jersey mannerisms and accent, I said, "Watchya do that for?!"

Luther calmly stated, "I don't know. Guess I wanted to see what would happen."

Yes, you too have people like Luther in your organization. Over the years I've had the opportunity to work with many like him and they require hefty doses of patience on our part. Individuals like Luther generally have a big heart, resembling Cousin Eddie from the movie *Christmas Vacation.* But our patience can only go so far and there are times when it becomes necessary to let Luther and Eddie go.

4 *We May Not Get Along in the Station, But . . .* Unhealthy Team Conflict

"Behold, how good and how pleasant it is For brethren to dwell together in unity!"

— Psalm 133:1

I have been in the fire service for thirty-six years. During that time I have had the opportunity to see a lot, do a lot, and hear a lot in both emergency and non-emergency situations. One statement I have often heard is, "We may not get along in the fire station, but when the call comes in we function very well on the street."

Many of you work in a team environment, and if you do not recognize the true meaning of the previous statement, I can tell you it comes in many forms at your local market: it is called bologna! People who cannot get along with one another create an atmosphere of disunity. Imagine driving on the interstate and a small rock bounces into your windshield, producing a chip and crack. As time passes the crack lengthens and grows larger. The small chip and crack eventually become a fractured windshield. Disunity has the same impact on families, friendships, and organizations: fracturing.

Workers report that thirty-one percent of their on-the-job stress is related to people.[3] Strife between team workers is manifested in frustration leading to anger, backbiting, gossip, hatred, bitterness, and discord. Dissension among coworkers also creates physical complications and mental stress, while often contributing to a lack of sleep, emotional duress, a decrease in productivity, missed work, etc.[4] In January 2015, *Forbes* reported that healthcare costs in the United States related to workplace stress were $190 billion.[5] Organizations exhibiting characteristics like these will not be found in a list of top twenty companies to work for. However, you will find them on the top fifty list of the ICI, also known as the infamous, contemptible, and infernal work environments.

The conditions described in the previous paragraph are unhealthy and destroy unity. Furthermore, team members are apt to devote more time to finding a way out of the situation than working productively. When not searching the internet for another job, they plan for Friday night and the weekend. Sunday night is hated because the evil cycle of disunity and fighting begins again on Monday.

Who wants to live in a world like that? Yet thousands of people do it week in and week out, year after year. The reasons why people remain in these toxic environments is beyond the scope of this book. Let us look at the underlying reason why a fractured workplace exists in the first place. Pure and simple, the explanation rests in the glaring absence of leadership.

In order for unity to exist within a team, the leader must address conflict. Failing to do so only allows the crack in the windshield to grow bigger. Before we delve into handling these issues, we will look at two examples of intra-team conflict. The first occurred during the American Civil War and the second inside an average neighborhood firehouse in the mid-1990s. You will see that little has changed regarding human behavior over the years.

TEAM CONFLICT DURING THE CIVIL WAR

We can glean many leadership lessons from a study of the Civil War. Among those is the amount of personal conflict that existed between many officers on both sides of the war, and the often tragic consequences that came with it. One example took place within the Union Army of the Potomac, ultimately leading to the death and injury of thousands of soldiers in the small Pennsylvania town of Gettysburg in July 1863.

In May of 1863, the Confederate Army of Northern Virginia, commanded by General Robert E. Lee, defeated the Union Army of the Potomac led by Major General Joseph "Fighting Joe" Hooker at Chancellorsville, Virginia. On May 6, "Fighting Joe" retreated across the Rappahannock River, creating alarm and anguish for President Abraham Lincoln.[6] The fact was, Hooker wasn't only at war with the Confederates, he was also embroiled in conflict with Lincoln and Major General Henry Halleck, who commanded the overall Union army.

Less than a month after the Battle of Chancellorsville, the Army of Northern Virginia marched north on June 3, intending to invade Pennsylvania. Hooker's strained relationship with his bosses began to take on even greater proportions.[7] What followed next was an arrogant, egotistical tantrum: Hooker wrote Lincoln a letter of resignation with the intention of trying to get his way like a three-year-old boy threatening to hold his breath if he does not get more candy. Fortunately, neither Lincoln nor Halleck gave into Hooker's demands; they accepted his resignation. However, "Fighting Joe" had allies, and in less than a week one of them would raise his head, fuel the fire of team conflict on the battlefield, and contribute to a controversy that is still debated today.

In the early morning hours of June 28, 1863, outside of Frederick, Maryland, an unsuspecting Major General George G. Meade was woken by a courier from Halleck to inform Meade that he was the new commanding General of the Army of the Potomac. Prior to this message, Meade commanded the Union Fifth Corps. Aside from his own Corps, he did not know the location or disposition of other Union commands, nor did Meade know where the Army of Northern Virginia was or what they were doing. Trying circumstances indeed for the fifth commanding General of the Army of the Potomac.

As Meade wrapped his arms around the military situation and planned his next moves, both armies came together in the fields and rolling hills west of Gettysburg on July 1. After heavy fighting throughout that first day, the Confederates eventually pushed the Army of the Potomac through Gettysburg and into the now-famous Union fishhook that extended from Culp's Hill through Cemetery Hill, south along Cemetery Ridge, and down into the Round Tops.

July 2 brought another day of ferocious combat between the North and South, but it would also be a day when intra-team conflict erupted within the higher ranks of the Union army—between Meade and Major General Daniel Sickles, the commanding general of the Third Corps.

Sickles was a man of dubious character with a tarnished reputation and political ambitions. He had served as a congressman from the State of New York and was associated with the infamous Tammany Hall Democrats. While a member of Congress, Sickles shot and killed Philip Barton Key (the son of Francis Scott Key, composer of *The Star-Spangled Banner*) for having an affair with his wife. After a trial by jury, Sickles was subsequently found not guilty due to temporary insanity. At the outbreak of the Civil War, Sickles recruited volunteer soldiers for the war and ultimately received a commission as a brigadier general.[8] His appointment to that rank was based on political favoritism and not military experience or merit. These facts contributed to the animosity between Sickles and many of his peers, including Meade.

Although Sickles had proved himself in combat, he was far from being a professional officer and soldier. His poor reputation became even more sullied after Hooker took command of the Army of the Potomac. Many complained that Hooker, Sickles, and Major General Daniel Butterfield had turned headquarters into a bar and a house of ill repute.[9] None of that sat well with Meade. After Meade assumed command of the Army of the Potomac, his dislike for Sickles continued to grow. On June 29, 1863, Meade openly criticized Sickles for not properly handling his supply trains and for the slow movement of the Third Corps.[10]

In the afternoon of July 2, 1863, Meade ordered Sickles to place the Third Corps to the left of Major General Winfield Hancock's Second Corps on Cemetery Ridge, thereby extending the Union line south to the Round Tops. Sickles did not like the assigned position and believed a better one existed along the Emmitsburg Road to the west. Without General Meade's permission, Sickles directed his men to move forward to the position of his choosing. Earlier in the afternoon, Meade had ordered Sickles to attend a meeting at headquarters, but Sickles had refused, citing the need to take care of other matters. Meade then sent his son, Captain Meade, to summon Sickles to the meeting, but Sickles refused to speak with him. Ultimately, General Meade rode forward to speak with Sickles, to order him to return the Third Corps to the place where they were most needed. However, it was too late, as the Confederates launched their attack against the Union lines.

The officers and enlisted men of the Third Corps paid for the disobedience and insubordination of Daniel Sickles with their lives. Harry W. Pfanz wrote, "Sickles's two divisions reported 593 officers and enlisted men killed, 3,029 wounded, and 589 missing."[11] It would be foolish on my part to attribute these casualties solely to the intra-team conflict that existed between George Meade and Daniel Sickles, but in hindsight the question must be asked: if the conflict had not existed and Sickles had obeyed orders, would the casualties have been just as high? That is a question many before me have pondered and one that I cannot answer. Later in the chapter, we will look into the leadership implications of the conflict between Meade and Sickles.

TEAM CONFLICT IN A NEIGHBORHOOD FIREHOUSE

Fortunately for the majority of people reading this book, the consequences of intra-team conflict will not be as tragic as those that occurred in Gettysburg. The type of conflict you will experience will be more along the lines of the following example. Several years ago, my hobby was taking pictures of fire trucks, and one Saturday my friend and I visited a fire department that had experienced a recent merger. For the sake of illustration, I will refer to them as Fire Department A and Fire Department B, but a more apt description would be the I Hate You Fire Department and the You Can Drop Dead Fire Department. The station we were visiting and the fire engine inside had belonged to the former Fire Department A and still reflected that in the name on the building and the fire engine.

We were greeted by two men who had belonged to Fire Department B. They still wore the badge and patch of that particular organization. We introduced ourselves and told them the purpose of our visit. They both said the truck belonged to Fire Department A and they would get the driver. After a few minutes passed, that person emerged from the station wearing the badge and patch of his former organization. He was a very friendly man, but also a very lonely and bitter one. He began to tell us about the problems associated with the merger and the negative impact it was having on him. The captain and firefighter in the station would not speak to him unless it was official business. They would not include him in the meals, and they controlled the television on their downtime. What a miserable environment for that man to work in for a twenty-four-hour shift!

No doubt the citizens of the jurisdiction assumed all was well within the four walls of that firehouse, and they certainly expected the crew to respond to any emergency and handle it efficiently and in a professional manner. The cold hard truth of the matter is this: when the three of them were not getting along in the fire station, there was absolutely no way they would perform as a cohesive team on the scene of whatever emergency they had to deal with.

I do not know all of the details taking place with the merger between those two departments, but someone clearly failed to handle the problem in that fire station. Not only was the conflict unprofessional, but it was also extremely juvenile in nature. The captain was the officer in charge of the crew, and he had allowed whatever discontent he had related to the merger to boil over into the station. He was not a leader—rather, he was an accomplice to rebellion and he was fueling the flames of hatred toward the members of Fire Department A. Fortunately, I am happy to report that ultimately the merger was successful and that particular fire department now functions as one organization.

LEADERSHIP IN SITUATIONS OF CONFLICT

Where was the leadership in both of these examples? Why didn't General Halleck exercise more control over his subordinates and attempt to get them to work together as a team? What were the chief officers in the merged fire department doing or not doing to address the conflict taking place in the fire stations? As leaders we have an obligation to address intra-team conflict. However, there are far too many people in positions of authority who sound like Sergeant Shultz from the 1960s television show

Hogan's Heroes, who repeatedly said, "I see nothing! I hear nothing!" When the Sergeant Shultz's of the world make statements like that, nothing gets fixed and everything gets worse.

You will notice I referred to people in positions of *authority* and not positions of *leadership*. That is because a leader will confront the problem and a manager will turn the other way hoping the situation will correct itself. It is no different than having a cavity in your tooth. The cavity will not get better on its own and unless you go to the dentist to get it fixed, you will be in a lot of pain.

The mission statement of the Loveland Fire Rescue Authority is, "Through commitment, compassion, and courage, the mission of the Loveland Fire Rescue Authority is to protect life and property."[12] There are many other organizations in the world using the word "courage" in their mission statements. However, simply writing phrases in a strategic plan, plastering them on the side of vehicles, or etching them on hallway plaques does not automatically mean everyone possesses the courage to approach someone and confront the issues at hand. Mission and vision statements and company slogans are great. But unless backed up with courageous action, they are mere words, only used during times of political necessity. Make no mistake, you *will* need courage, discernment, and wisdom to confront the problems existing between people on your team.

Leaders will step forward and grab the bull by the horns. They acknowledge the task of confronting people is distasteful and filled with stress and uncertainty. But they recognize it as a necessary duty that must be done. Failing to do anything less allows the cracks in the windshield to grow.

As a chief officer and shift commander, I appreciate and support the individuals who have the mettle and intestinal fortitude to meet personnel issues head-on and work toward resolution. Generally they are people who understand the concept of handling problems at the lowest possible level. Remember that leadership is not connected to positions of authority. I firmly believe this approach keeps most personnel issues small and manageable. In other words, "Head 'em off at the pass, Clem!" Many intra-team conflicts can be handled by individuals who are not in supervisory positions. This is accomplished through conversations or peer pressure. Colonel Bryan P. McCoy (USMC) refers to this as "The Virtue of Shame." He writes, "Shame is the knowledge that one's behavior or performance is less than what is expected by the group. Shame in the eyes of our brothers is a powerful motivator. No one wants to be known or remembered for coming up short when most needed."[13]

I want to acknowledge there may be times when the situation is dire enough that you have to separate the parties involved and send someone home. Also, in the day and age in which we live, with workplace violence being an unfortunate reality, if threats have been made or the conflict has turned physical, more than likely a law enforcement agency will become involved. Dealing with those particular circumstances is beyond the scope of this book; assistance can be found in the realm of safety and security experts.

Understand that some organizations in the world require employees to run everything by a supervisor first, including reporting emergencies. I have seen this more than one time during my career and the emergency never, never gets better under those types of procedures. The employee wedged under the truck is still stuck and dying, the employee having chest pains is getting worse and having more difficulty breathing, and the fire is getting bigger. The employee who is threatening someone or brandishing a weapon will not stop after three supervisors have been notified via the telephone that there's a problem. You must be familiar with your organizational policies and procedures, but also exercise common sense and get the appropriate help to the incident. And sometimes help comes in the form of a person with a badge and gun, driving a fast, black-and-white car.

CONFRONTING THE CONFLICT

Let us return to the taxing intra-team conflict that needs to be addressed, but does not have a violent, or potentially violent, component. The problem may have just arisen, you may have inherited the conflict, or positive peer pressure has been nonexistent or not working. The list of possibilities is endless, but the problem must be handled by someone with leadership ability. How?

To begin with, do not jump to conclusions. This can be very damaging to innocent parties and to you. Alford L. McMichael recommends "I over E," or intelligence over emotion.[14] I certainly agree, but I also want to consider the biblical perspective from Proverbs 18:13, "He who answers a matter before he hears it, It is folly and shame to him." Similarly, in Proverbs 10:19 we find "In the multitude of words sin is not lacking, But he who restrains his lips is wise." Take a deep breath, step back, ask questions, and determine what is actually taking place before you react. And yes, many times that is much easier said than done.

It is vitally important to avoid making assumptions based on your initial gut reaction, because you might be wrong. You also need to be careful that you are not swayed by others or by your personal opinion and/or biases about the individuals involved. I have not only been caught in that trap, but I have been on the receiving end of assumptions. Neither spot is good. In the former circumstances, I put myself in a position where I needed to go back and apologize for not thoroughly looking into the matter, and passing judgment before I had all of the facts. When I have been the recipient of suppositions, it only upset me and made me question the overall motives of what was taking place.

There is another important fact to remember. Because someone has been in trouble in the past or they have been difficult to work with, does not automatically make them the guilty party. Every organization has the fair-haired golden children, the Prince or Princess who can do no wrong, and some of those people are very adept at making others look bad. In my experience, the Prince and Princess are usually intent on climbing to the top, and they don't care who gets stepped on or bowled over in the process. Therefore, if they are the source of the team conflict, and they can make it look like the person with the bad reputation is the guilty party, then the Prince and Princess will influence the circumstances in their favor. Beware of this condition, exercise sound discernment, and do not get sucked into their manipulative snares.

Hopefully you are employed in an organization where you can seek advice on how to handle the situation if you need it. If that is not possible, seek guidance from other trusted sources. A good reference I have used is *Crucial Conversations: Tools for Talking When Stakes Are High.*[15] You also need to know organizational policies and procedures, and what internal resources are available to you. However, it by no means indicates you are escalating this to an issue involving superiors or the Human Resources Department. It simply means you know what procedures are in place in the event the team conflict cannot be resolved at your level.

Once the facts have been gathered and prior to meeting with the parties concerned, develop a game plan on how you are going to address the matter. The plan should include the end state, i.e., what do you want the outcome to look like?[16] How is the desired outcome going to be reached, and how are you going to hold the individuals accountable as you move forward? The latter includes periodic follow-up meetings to ensure the issue has truly been resolved, to show each person involved that there is an accountability piece to the process, and to demonstrate that as the leader you are truly concerned with what is going on.

Your plan should include ground rules for a structured meeting, but at the same time, avoid stifling the conversation. At the start of the meeting, share the rules and let them know the conversation will be civilized and personal attacks will not be allowed. As you listen to the comments, make sure you can sift through the differences between facts and emotions.

My wife has counseled a number of women over the years, and one of the many things I have learned from her is emotions are *real* but they are not *authoritative*. For example, I recently attended a meeting and at the conclusion, I wanted to introduce myself to a colleague I had never met before in another organization. His back was to me, he was positioned close to the door, and as he was leaving the room, I wanted to catch him before someone else did. At the same time, I noticed a coworker in my peripheral vision, whom I ignored for the moment. I was able to catch up with the person I wanted to meet and a few minutes later I saw my coworker again. He said, "I thought you were mad at me." When I asked why, he said that as I passed him in the room, he had said hello and I ignored him. My coworker made an assumption based on feelings. His feelings were real, but they were not authoritative—I was focused on introducing myself to the other person. You need to be alert to these types of feelings and get to the facts.

During the meeting, take notes of what is said. If it does become necessary to document the situation in a performance evaluation or the matter escalates to a progressive disciplinary process, you will want to refer to notes and not rely on your memory. In regard to taking notes, when I am dealing with a personnel issue I always use a separate piece of paper that I can put into a folder rather than using my notebook. Why? If the dispute turns into a legal matter and my folder is subpoenaed, I'm not missing important project or meeting information like I would be if my notebook were in the hands of a lawyer.

MEETING RECAP AND FOLLOW-UP

At the conclusion of the meeting, recap what was said and ensure the parties involved know they will be held accountable. To hold people responsible, you must set expectations and goals for them to accomplish. Also, establish a timeframe for follow-up meetings. I recommend you base the frequency on two things: the severity of the issue and the response of the individuals involved during the meeting. A less severe issue and favorable reaction will not require as much follow-up as more serious problems with negative responses.

Do not be misled into thinking one meeting will take care of everything! When we are dealing with human beings and their emotions, those problems are not as easily corrected as changing a flat tire on your car. Especially if the conflict has been taking place for a number of years.

Remember to keep your immediate supervisor informed of what is taking place. As a boss I don't need to know every detail, but I also don't want to be taken off guard if the matter does not get resolved.

How will you know if the situation does not get better? My experience has shown that intra-team conflict is often invisible.

The parties involved may put on a show and attempt to deceive you, while they continue the poor behavior behind your back. So keep your eyes and ears open and watch for cues and clues from other people on the team. For example, watch how they react with each other in conversations, listen for snide or sarcastic comments, and pay attention to body language. Even if the individuals involved are smiling politicians in your presence, sooner or later, if you are paying attention, you will see the truth come to light.

In the event the matter is not resolved, you must take the next steps of correction. Depending on organizational policies, this could range from a verbal warning up to termination. As I stated earlier, you must be familiar with established procedures and seek help.

The chapter began with a statement I have heard more than once in my career: "We may not get along in the fire station, but when the call comes in we function very well on the street." You may not work in a firehouse, but unless you're self-employed and the company is called Lone Wolf Guru, then you are working in a team environment. Intra-team conflict creates problems for everyone and does not equate to the professional and efficient delivery of service.

Remember that unhealthy conflict and unity cannot coexist in the same sentence. However, *healthy* conflict can help strengthen the unity of your team and organization. Proverbs 27:17 says, "As iron sharpens iron, So a man sharpens the countenance of his friend." From that standpoint think of a busy railroad line. The friction between the locomotive and railcars with the track creates a bright, shiny, useful surface. Contrast that with an abandoned rail line: the tracks are rusty and of little good anymore other than scrap metal. As a leader, have the courage to address the intra-team conflict so your organizational rails will be bright, shiny, and useful.

Practical Application

- Questions are not an automatic indicator of unhealthy conflict. Dwight D. Eisenhower said, "May we never confuse honest dissent with disloyal subversion." Know the difference!
- Intra-team conflict requires deliberate, courageous action by the leader.
- Do your part as a leader to create a healthy working environment to reduce stress, increase morale, and enhance productivity.
- Gain an understanding of human behavior, and exercise discernment to separate emotions from facts.
- Know and understand your organizational policies and procedures, and keep your immediate supervisor informed.
- Pay attention to people's behavior. Eventually someone involved in the conflict will open up to a friend and spill their guts. Others will also notice body language, snide comments, aloofness, etc. Proverbs 27:23 states, "Be diligent to know the state of your flocks, And attend to your herds."

Esprit de Corps

The opposite of unhealthy team conflict is *esprit de corps*, a French phrase denoting "the spirit of the corps."

After being honorably discharged from the Air Force, my motivation for joining the Marine Corps was twofold. I desired to return to firefighting and I wanted to be part of the best fighting organization in the world. Initially I enlisted into the Marine Corps Reserve. After my first drill weekend, I knew I had found what I was looking for. In less than six months I entered active duty through the prior service/other service program, with orders to report to Marine Corps Air Station Yuma, Arizona, as a firefighter.

My firefighting exploits in the Marine Corps did not last long. Less than three months after reporting to Yuma, I was informed there were too many NCOs (noncommissioned officers) in crash crew. Consequently, there was a need to re-train into another MOS (military occupational specialty). The career planner shoved a large, three-ring binder into my hands with a "dream sheet" on top and said, "Pick three jobs." For those not familiar with the "dream sheet," it's a form the service member completes listing desired jobs or locations where you would like to be stationed. In other words, you are dreaming if you think you'll get what you want.

I flipped through the pages of the binder and selected three careers that interested me. My first choice was the intelligence field because of skills and knowledge that could transfer to the civilian world. My second option was a combat engineer. There were transferrable skills, but I relished the idea of building and/or demolishing things in a military environment. My third choice was armor. The notion of riding in an M-61 Abrams tank while firing the main gun had a certain appeal to it.

I wrote my choices on the infamous dream sheet and waited. In less than a month my answer came back. I stared at the orders in disbelief. My new MOS was an Aviation Operations Specialist. The dream sheet had earned its name.

Aviation operations was a stark contrast to the world of firefighting. I no longer worked in a fire station, but an office. Responsibilities included working with flight data, pilot log books, and a multitude of administrative functions. I also learned two valuable skills that remain with me to this day: typing and computers. Admittedly, in the moment I did not place too much value on those skills, but little did I realize how important they would be in the future.

One day in the spring of 1986, my boss, Gunny Rosemond, asked if I was interested in deploying to Norway in September with another squadron. Norway!? Of course I said yes. Then came a sunny, hot, humid day in August when I returned to work from lunch and was told to report to the commanding officer (CO), Lieutenant Colonel Capito. I thought, "Uh-oh! What have I done to skip over the Gunny and sergeant major and report directly to the CO?" There is a very strict chain of command in the Marine Corps, and the sequence was out of place. I racked my brain trying to figure out why the colonel wanted to see me.

I was told to stand at ease and he said, "Pack your trash, Davis, you're going to Norway." I told him the Gunny previously passed on information about the September deployment. He matter-of-factly said, "No, you're leaving in the morning. Go across the street to Group, get your orders, then go to Supply and get your gear." I was being temporarily assigned to S-3 Operations with the Fourth Marine Amphibious Brigade (MAB) on board the USS Mount Whitney, a command and control ship. Twenty-four hours later I was in Norfolk, Virginia, requesting permission to board the ship.

We were participating in a large military exercise called Northern Wedding/Bold Guard 1986. I had the time of my life. I loved being at sea and even more, I loved my assignment with the 4th MAB. I was privileged to work with outstanding officers who were some of the finest leaders I ever associated with. They not only lived the Marine Corps leadership principles and traits, but they were also great examples. The esprit de corps within the 4th MAB was the best I experienced in the military. The morale was high and the comradeship was tight. The desire to accomplish the mission was present with everyone I worked with. This was evident on board the Mount Whitney and ashore in both Norway and northern Germany. The spirit among everyone drove us to excel at our jobs and spurred us to accomplish tasks not asked of us. In the field, we worked a twelve-hour shift in the combat operations center (COC) and then another four hours sitting in a hole with an M-60 machine gun.

We did not complain about the hours, the type of duty, or the leaders we worked for. Why? Because of esprit de corps: unity, cohesion, and our sense of duty to the Marine Corps and the nation. Because this was a temporary duty assignment, my time with the 4th MAB eventually came to an end just as abruptly as my initial assignment. The sergeant major walked into the COC and told me I was going back to Cherry Point with one of the pilots. My protests were to no avail as he told me I had reached the end of my time with them. Forty-eight hours later I was back in North Carolina, and I did not want to be there. I missed the bonds and comradeship of the 4th MAB. I missed the exemplary leadership of the officers. I missed the importance of what we were doing. The 4th MAB was a healthy organization and I wanted to work there and be part of the unit. After all, don't we all want to experience esprit de corps and unity at work?

5 *I Know Who You Are* Shedding Bias Toward Subordinates

"To be a critic, you have to have maybe 3 percent education, 3 percent intelligence, 2 percent style, and 90 percent gall and egomania in equal parts."

—Judith Crist, Film Critic

Judith Crist's quote can be equally applied to the nitpickers in our lives. When we demonstrate a bias toward another person, we have elevated ourselves to the position of a faultfinder, and all too frequently a detractor as well. How often is our bias based on the differences between us? Topping the list are political, racial, ethnic, cultural, religious, and gender issues. But what about other types of prejudice we carry with us? Without considering the previous list, how do you view the people who clean your office, change your oil, wait on your table at the restaurant, or those doing hundreds of other jobs a lot of people would not want to do?

Bias toward others appears in a number of different ways. Have you ever heard of the term "Shoobie?" That's a word used by Jersey Shore locals for the summer visitors who flock to the boardwalk and beach wearing tennis shoes and socks, or worse yet, sandals and socks.[17] At one of my duty stations in the military, there was a staff sergeant from Alabama. He never called me by my name and rank, it was always, "Hey, Yankee!" Apparently he never realized that he was in the United States Air Force and not the Confederate Air Force. In college I wrote a paper titled *East versus West.* It was a short analysis of the cultural differences between the two coasts of our country. There are no two ways about it: ill-conceived perceptions are alive and well. Let's take a look at what happens when accusations are leveled at a subordinate based on reputation and hearsay evidence, without knowing anything at all or very little about that person.

The history of the Loveland Fire Rescue Authority (LFRA) traces back to 1883. In 1912, the first paid employee was hired.[18] Today, with the exception of a small volunteer force in a mountainous area of the jurisdiction, the rest of the personnel are paid employees. However, when I first joined the department in 1990, there were only two paid people working in a fire station: the officer (either a captain or lieutenant in charge) and an engineer (the person driving and operating the vehicle). The remainder of the workforce consisted of volunteer firefighters responding from work or home to the scene of an emergency. During my earlier years with the department, the paid employees had quite a bit of input regarding shift and fire station selection, and also who we wanted to work with—although there were times when none of those options came together as desired. Such was my case in the late 1990s.

EXTREME PREJUDICE

In 1997 I was a lieutenant in charge of an LFRA fire station on the west side of the city and quite content with the shift, the station, and my driver, Floyd. In autumn of that year, there was a meeting of all the paid employees to complete the selection process previously described. We were on duty that day and all started out well. That is, until Floyd and I were dispatched to an emergency. Returning to the selection process after the emergency, I walked into the room and was stunned to see what took place in our absence. I was no longer on the same shift nor in the same station, I wasn't working with Floyd anymore, and I had a different captain. (As a side note, during that period of time our shift commanders were captains, but that changed in mid-2003 when the position became a battalion chief.)

I was shocked because of the captain I had been assigned to. Other than working some overtime shifts together, we had never been permanently assigned to the same shift. A few years after being hired, I developed a distrust of this individual for various reasons. However, I naively held to the belief that perhaps it wouldn't be so bad working for him. That notion came to a grinding halt on January 24, 1998. I specifically remember the day because it was Super Bowl Sunday, when the Denver Broncos played the Green Bay Packers. Prior to the start of the game, our captain came to the fire station to lay out his expectations for the shift.

When the captain finished the meeting he looked at me and said, "I want to talk to you in the truck bay." So we went to the other side of the station where no one could see us and he said, "I know who you are and I know what you are about." He then proceeded to tell me what kind of a troublemaker I was, along with several other false accusations attacking my character. When he finally quit talking, I said, "So that's the way it's going to be, huh?" The captain told me it *was* going to be that way and he left the station.

Why was he biased toward me? After all, we had only been on the same shift since January 1. My speculation is that most of his predisposition was based on the reputation I had gained. When I saw people who I believed were unethical, power-hungry, driven by personal gain, controlling, politically motivated, and so on, I would say something. As a matter of fact, I still speak up when I see those kinds of people; I just try to be smarter in how I handle the situation.

What happened in that fire station on January 24? The Bible explains it this way in Proverbs 18:13: "He who answers a matter before he hears it, It is folly and shame to him." Rather than seeking to understand and attempting to find out what kind of a person I truly was, the captain came out of the gate and launched into threats and weak attempts at intimidation, neither of which have ever worked with me. So I dug in my heels and what little respect and trust I had for this individual completely evaporated and never returned. I have had some rough years in my life, but 1998 and 1999 rank toward the top. Unfortunately, there were times during those two years when I contributed to the tension between myself and the captain. I dealt with a lot of anger back then, and more than one time my resentment boiled over, creating more problems.

Fortunately, I addressed my anger a couple of years later and the lessons I learned on this issue will be detailed in Chapter 6.

The friction between myself and the captain peaked in October 1999 during Fire Prevention Week. I had taken part of the shift off to attend my daughter's piano recital, so I wasn't present during the open house at my fire station. A week later I received a late-night email from the captain accusing me of not allowing a civilian and her son inside the firehouse. First of all, I did not remember that occurring, and second, it was an absurd allegation as I had always allowed people inside the station for tours. However, he was adamant it was me and even went so far as to say, "I know it's you because she said it was a short guy with glasses and you're the only short guy with glasses on the fire department!"

As a result of this situation, a meeting was scheduled between the fire chief, the captain, and me. During the meeting, I was not asked what had taken place and I was not allowed to defend myself against the false claim. I quickly viewed the meeting as a kangaroo court where the verdict had been predetermined before I walked into the room. The chief and captain pronounced me guilty and neither one was interested in what I had to say. Even though I was not guilty, I offered to personally give Suzette and her son a tour of the fire station. When I left the meeting with the fire chief and captain, I was completely demoralized, and if there had been an opportunity for me to take a job with another fire department, I would have done so.

The next morning I called Suzette to arrange a tour of the station the following Saturday. When she arrived at the station with her son Billy, my first thought was, "I've never seen this person before in my life." Furthermore, Suzette had a confused and quizzical look on her face that indicated, "Who is this guy?" I showed Billy the firehouse and gave him a ride on the fire engine. The tour went well, and Suzette and her son expressed their gratitude for the opportunity to visit and learn more about firefighters.

Most reasonable people would assume their boss would follow-up to see how the tour went. However, the captain never took the time to find out what happened during Suzette's visit. Due to the strained relationship with him, I felt that if he didn't care enough to ask then I had no desire to let him know. Looking back, I was wrong. Although his post-tour inaction displayed an apathetic attitude, I should have demonstrated the initiative and leadership to inform him of what took place during her visit.

Several weeks passed. I was called into the captain's office, where he said that Suzette had called him and she indicated the station tour went well. After hemming and hawing and stumbling over his words, the captain stated that the person who refused Suzette access to the station wasn't me; it was someone else. As a matter of fact, it was the individual driving for me at the time, but he never had the courage to speak up and take responsibility for his actions. My driver had made the unethical decision to allow me to take the fall for his rudeness and poor behavior toward Suzette. My captain was obviously embarrassed at the egregious error he had made in passing judgment without gathering all of the facts. I was exasperated, frustrated, and dumbfounded over the entire incident, and said to him, "I told you that it wasn't me!"

Since the false accusation had been levied against me the previous month, I had not wanted to go to work. I was discouraged and felt like a large target was placed on my back. Fortunately, the captain apologized, but our relationship never progressed beyond a lukewarm state. Two months later he moved into a different position in the fire department and we never worked together again. However, several years later during a meeting, my former captain admitted to others that he had been wrong and had jumped to conclusions about me. I too had been wrong in a number of areas.

A DIFFERENT RESPONSE

Let's return to the first incident on January 24, 1998. The captain failed to seek to understand, but instead of me coming across as a wise guy from Jersey with something to prove, what could I have done differently? After all, you and I are responsible for our actions, our words, and our behaviors—regardless of how another person treats us. For starters, I could have done something that was extremely difficult for me at that time in my life: keep my mouth shut. I should have heeded Proverbs 15:1, "A soft answer turns away wrath, But a harsh word stirs up anger," and verse 18, "A wrathful man stirs up strife, But he who is slow to anger allays contention." Also, I should have exercised Ephesians 4:32, "And be kind to one another, tenderhearted, forgiving one another, even as God in Christ forgave you." However, the hard lesson I needed to learn about anger was still another four years away.

Instead of me saying to him, "So that's the way it's going to be, huh?" I could have kept a civil tongue in my mouth and said, "Captain, your assumptions about me are incorrect. How about giving me a chance and you'll see I'm not the person you think I am?" However, that did not happen. Instead, I chose the path of "I'll show him!" My approach did nothing but add gasoline to an already unstable situation.

What did I learn from those two years in 1998 and 1999? For one, I don't always have to prove I'm right, and neither do you. Was my character attacked and my honor brought into question? Absolutely it was. Please understand I am not suggesting that we let people walk on us like a doormat. However, there is an appropriate way to respond in circumstances when we are verbally assaulted. Take a deep breath, try to remain calm, and do not allow your emotions to take over. Does that mean the situation won't escalate? Not necessarily, but we should strive to handle the attack in a respectful manner where we maintain our integrity, regardless of what the other person is saying or doing. It is very difficult to do, but rise above the situation and let the other person make an oaf of themselves. In the end we will be able to look ourselves and others in the eye and know we handled the matter correctly. Plus, you will have more credibility if and when the problem has to go up the chain of command.

Be careful about jumping to conclusions. Question the validity of reputations that people might have, including good reputations. Throughout my career there have been individuals who had "great" reputations as fire officers, but when the truth was revealed and you saw them beyond the scene of an emergency, they failed to exercise authority and leadership with their subordinates. Yes, they were courageous during emergencies and could make sound tactical decisions, but they were afraid to confront problems they should have been handling on a day-to-day basis. In the end, their reputation for being a good fire officer wasn't well-founded.

You may be wondering what happened to my driver who threw me under the bus in October 1999. The morning after I received the email accusing me of not allowing the civilian in the fire station, I asked him if he knew about it. He denied any knowledge and actually laid the blame on the lieutenant who covered my position while I was at the piano recital. When I asked that lieutenant if he recalled the event, he too denied any knowledge, and I had no doubt he was telling me the truth. I still suspected the person responsible for denying Suzette and her son access to the fire station was my driver. When I finally learned the guilty party was, in fact, my driver, I couldn't immediately confront him due to circumstances beyond my control. Eventually I spoke to him and voiced my displeasure at his lack of accountability, an absence of character on his part, his failure for not having the courage to take responsibility for what he did, and for allowing me to be the fall guy. As January 1, 2000, rolled around, I began the new millennium on a different shift, with a different supervisor, and with a different driver. Two of the worst years in my career as a firefighter had come to an end.

THE CONSEQUENCES OF EXTREME PREJUDICE

But why did this happen to begin with? Because the captain had a preconceived bias toward me.

Prior to us working together in January of 1998, he drew several conclusions about me based on rumors, his distant observations, and my reputation for being outspoken. But rather than making a concerted effort to find out whether any of the aforementioned was true, he took a forceful approach through threats and intimidation. He tried to manage me rather than lead me. In the 1979 movie *Apocalypse Now,* the character played by Martin Sheen was told to eliminate Colonel Walter E. Kurtz, played by Marlon Brando, with "extreme prejudice." What happens when you enter into a working relationship harboring extreme prejudice toward the other person? Count on nothing but problems for everyone concerned.

As leaders we need a better understanding of why some people develop bias and extreme prejudice toward others. The big-ticket items are related to race, color, ethnicity, religion, and gender. However, my experiences described in this chapter have nothing to do with any of those. My story revolves around reputation and rumors. Do we feel threatened by someone else because they have a reputation of being outspoken? Have we fallen into the trap of believing rumors and not seeking to understand the truth? Do we attempt to manage someone and mold them into our image rather than lead and develop them? Subordinates with a reputation can be threatening to those in positions of authority who lack leadership training and people skills. Does pride prevent us from seeking guidance on how to lead the difficult people we work with?

Leadership is much more than managing people as if they were boxes of paper cups. We cannot ignore those who have earned less-than-stellar reputations (whether true or not). At the same time, leadership does not put on the heavy, spiked metal glove and make assumptions based on rumors or misleading evidence.

One of the critical first steps in shelving a bias toward someone else is to obtain the facts and not allow our perceptions and emotions to take over and rule the day. That reaction accomplishes nothing more than creating tension and friction, not only between you and the individual concerned, but with those who are exposed to the situation as well, such as your family, friends, and coworkers.

Have you ever seen a video of what happens to someone when they are in the gym and they try to jump onto a large wooden box that is half their height and they miss? The unfortunate individual catches the edge of the box, causing it to tip toward them, and on the downward journey the amateur gymnast smashes their knees on the box, sustaining the first injury. Then as both they and the box obey the laws of gravity, the other part of the box smacks them in the face, usually drawing blood and possibly knocking out a few teeth. That is what happens to us when we engage in the frequently used exercise program of jumping to conclusions.

Practical Application

- Reflect (but don't dwell) on past events, analyze what happened, apply the lessons learned, and grow from the experience.
- If you are creating issues like the ones described in this chapter, then you need to ask yourself why.
- When you are verbally assaulted, control your emotions. However, at the same time, do not allow yourself to become a doormat for someone else's attacks.
- In the Marine Corps we affectionately referred to the mouth as the pie hole. So a large part of controlling our emotions revolves around keeping our pie hole shut. Psalms 141:3, "Set a guard, O Lord, over my mouth; Keep watch over the door of my lips."
- Setting aside our bias toward others does not mean we always have to agree on everything or hold the same beliefs.
- Those who cannot set aside differences and bias will have an extremely difficult time leading people. On April 22, 1800, Thomas Jefferson wrote to William Hamilton, "I never considered a difference of opinion in politics, in religion, in philosophy, as cause for withdrawing from a friend."[19]
- Ralph Waldo Emerson said, "All persons are puzzles until at last we find in some word or act the key to the man, to the woman; straightway all their past words and actions lie in light before us."[20]

Nicknames

Most people receive nicknames or assign nicknames to someone else. Growing up in Cedarville, New Jersey, I was dubbed "Slick." In high school, a small group referred to me as "Moon Dog." At Loveland Fire Rescue, I have been referred to as "Jersey Rick" (a title usually attached to me when I am more firm and vocal). Throughout the years I worked with various people holding nicknames such as Smiley, Colonel Klink, Uncle Fester, Ferret Face, Blinky the Clown, Landlord Larry, Cooter, and other names even less endearing.

Bosses and supervisors who fail to lead are tyrants, micromanagers, braggarts, and a host of other poor qualities—and are often given unflattering nicknames by their subordinates. Throughout my life I never saw anyone like this receive a positive nickname. These monikers are rarely based on objective or scientific criteria, but rather they are subjective opinions grounded on behaviors. At times a nickname is unfounded and unfair. The title was assigned by someone who had an ax to grind with a supervisor and the name took on a life of its own. In other words, the foundation for the name revolved around a bias toward the boss. Yet many times, the boss builds the bias toward themselves on their own.

Such is the case with a fire chief I worked for in the 1970s at a large military base. Each week in the fire station we watched *The Dukes of Hazzard.* It was a popular television show about two cousins, Bo and Luke Duke. Their zany, good-natured hijinks always outwitted the two antagonists, Sheriff Roscoe P. Coltrane and a corrupt politician named Boss Hogg. The local watering hole was called the Boar's Nest, which was conveniently owned by none other than Boss Hogg. Out of pure coincidence, our fire chief physically resembled Boss Hogg, so guess what? That was his nickname. We called his office the Boar's Nest. As with any legend, who knows when the chief earned the title, but he never did anything to help his cause.

Occasionally we were blessed to hear of the chief's amazing exploits as a firefighter. In one of his most memorable stories, he told us a jet bomber crashed into a million-gallon fuel storage tank and erupted in flames. He and another firefighter responded in a small fire truck and the two of them extinguished the fire, saving lives and protecting billions of taxpayer dollars. Truly a remarkable event that a grateful nation is thankful for and certainly worthy of the highest recognition. Especially in light of the fact that a large, eight-engine jet bomber with eight people on board crashing into that much fuel would ignite a massive fire beyond the capabilities of one small fire engine. No, I wasn't at the crash, but the details are questionable. After the fire chief left the room I saw firefighters reaching across their shoulder, patting themselves on the back, imitating the chief's voice, and speaking about extinguishing a large bomber fire in a million-gallon fuel tank.

The possibility exists the chief was aware of his nickname, because he began to make rare appearances on Sunday nights to conduct training exercises. After one such training drill on a weekday, we all gathered in the dayroom to discuss what we did well and what needed to be corrected. As we filed into the room, the shift commander was at the front having a discussion with the station captain about the drill. Unbeknownst to the station captain, Boss Hogg slipped into the back of the room and sat down.

My friend Russ was seated next to me, and he must have possessed incredible intuition that something was going to go terribly wrong. Russ made several futile attempts to get the attention of the station captain, who was becoming more animated and vocal about the drills. The shift commander was standing behind a podium, and he began to nervously rock the pedestal back and forth. Obviously, he too could see the dam was about to burst.

All of a sudden the station captain blurted out, "When are we going to have another one of these drills!?"

The shift commander sheepishly asked, "What drills?" To which the station captain in full force and determination stated, "You know! Boss Hogg's drills!"

From the back of the room, the fire chief thundered, "What was that!? What was my name!?"

The shift commander at the podium turned pale and looked like he was going to pass out. The station captain, meanwhile, turned and nonchalantly said, "I was wondering when we were going to have another one of your drills." There was an ignition that morning and it wasn't a bomber crashing into fuel tanks. The fire chief stormed out of the room. I mustered all my strength to suppress the laughter, knowing if I uttered one sound I would be in trouble.

At the conclusion of the after-action review (AAR), both the shift commander and station captain were summoned to the Boar's Nest. One by one, we took turns creeping to a vantage point and glancing into the chief's office to see what was going on. I will never forget what I saw. The chief had a secretary, but he was hunched over a typewriter with two fingers banging away at the keys. I surmised Boss Hogg was typing a written warning for the station captain. Not long afterward, the recipient of the written warning took all of us to the back of the fire station for a counseling session. He was angry and red-faced. The station captain's pointed finger resembled a bayonet attached to a rifle. He parried and thrust his finger back and forth and threatened to kill the next man who called the chief Boss Hogg or his office the Boar's Nest.

Nicknames can be endearing. Nicknames can be demeaning. Nicknames may be unjustly earned based on bias. Nicknames can take on a life of their own. User beware. Ecclesiastes 10:20 reads, "Do not curse the king, even in your thought; Do not curse the rich, even in your bedroom; For a bird of the air may carry your voice, And a bird in flight may tell the matter." In this story, the bird was a grown man, and he roosted in the wrong nest.

6 *You Keep Breaking the Glass* The Consuming Fire of Anger

"Anger is momentary madness, so control
your passion or it will control you."

— Horace, Roman Poet

Sunday, September 11, 2011, was the tenth anniversary of the terrorist attacks on the United States. It was a beautiful, clear night when my wife Debbie and I left the house to pick up our daughter from a church activity in nearby Fort Collins. We were less than two miles from our house when I received notification of a large hazardous materials incident at the intersection of U.S. Highway 34 and Interstate 25. Then several text messages appeared on my phone in quick succession indicating a large emergency was unfolding. We were northwest of the interchange and driving east with a clear view toward the direction of the incident. In the distance I saw an orange glow lighting up the night sky. Even in the dark, a large, black cloud of smoke was clearly visible billowing above the fire. I also received a text message directing off-duty personnel to return to work.

At Loveland Fire Rescue Authority, the chief officers are assigned a staff vehicle to take home so we can be available for on-call duty and response to off-duty emergencies when required. This was one of those situations where I needed to respond. As I turned east on U.S. Highway 34, there was no mistaking the location of the incident as the fire loomed large and bright in front of me. Arriving on scene, I saw a gasoline tanker lying on its side, fully engulfed in flames. The adjacent light pole was starting to bend and fall to the ground because of the impinging fire. I reported to the command post and was assigned the position of incident safety officer.

Before I assumed my duties, the incident commander informed me the driver of the truck had not been able to escape and he had perished in the accident.

The truck had been traveling north on I-25 and exited eastbound on U.S. Highway 34. As the vehicle was turning, it rolled over onto the driver's side of the truck cab. Witnesses reported the driver did not appear to be moving. Before anyone could reach him, a fire erupted, consuming the aluminum tank containing approximately nine thousand gallons of gasoline. Based on the location of the truck and an obvious death, a unified decision was made between Loveland Fire and the Colorado State Patrol to let the fuel burn off. In the end, that course of action was less hazardous to everyone, as it eliminated the necessity of handling large quantities of dangerous, unburned gasoline and lessened the potential for environmental damage.

Even from a safe distance, the intense heat produced by the raging fire forced my head down in order to shield my face. My eyes tend to be light-sensitive and the flames burned bright enough to compel me to squint. The inferno also produced a loud roaring sound, accompanied by large billowing clouds of black smoke laced with reddish-orange flames. Both I-25 and U.S. 34, two major highways in Northern Colorado, were closed because of the incident. Traffic backed up for miles as the orange glow attracted people from the surrounding area who were wondering what was going on. Tragically, the driver lost his life, but fortunately, no one else was injured or killed. I have been to a lot of fires throughout my career. That one will be etched into my memory for a long time.

RICK'S INFERNO

The gasoline tanker fire was like the anger burning in me at one time. A fury that would erupt and cause people to shield their faces and ears, not knowing what I was going to say or do. I roared, sending billows of smoke skyward, letting everyone know I was upset. Many times it did not take much to set my gasoline on fire.

Later I would attempt to justify the anger by saying, "That's just the way I am."

What caused me to always be at a simmer, just a few degrees below the boiling point? Several things probably contributed to my deep-seated anger.

The Davis family is short in stature and one year before starting grade school, Dad issued a warning that I would have to defend myself because of it. You know what? He was right. Several times in grade school, bullies picked on me for not only being short, but also for wearing glasses. I allowed their actions to go to a certain point before throwing a punch, bringing things to a quick end. I recognized a solution that worked for me: get angry, strike fast, strike hard, and overcome the foe by complete and total surprise.

Most of the time, my opponents turned into friends after they realized I would not stand for their bullying. Although the solution worked for me on the playground in the 1960s, we live in a different age where bullying is still very much alive but requires a smarter approach to squash than the one I used. The good news is that as I grew older and left grade school, I quit the fighting . . . but the wrath was still present below the surface.

Another contributing factor to my anger was the death of my dad when I was fourteen years old. Even though he had been in poor health for at least six years and I knew deep down that he would not live long, I became an angrier person after finding him on the floor, dead of a heart attack. In high school, my academic struggles with algebra, geometry, physics, and biology only exacerbated my frustration. The only thing I wanted to do was quit school, join the military, and become a firefighter. Thank God there was a man who lived next door to us who recognized what was going on in my life. That person was my Uncle Cliff, and he played an important role in keeping me in high school. Later in the book, I'll describe him in more detail, and how he helped me.

My senior year of high school, I saw the light of graduation at the end of the tunnel. I also grew more excited at the prospect of being a military firefighter after finishing school. However, I was so anxious to achieve my dream goal that I wasn't smart about my approach to enlisting in the military.

The Marine recruiter said there was no problem for me to enlist as a firefighter. On the other hand, the Air Force recruiter told me I could not join the service as a firefighter. However, he said I would be able to get my job changed to firefighting once I was at boot camp. At the time, my Uncle Kent was approaching twenty years in the Air Force. When I spoke to him about the Marine recruiter, my uncle said, "Rick, that Jarhead's lying to you!" I believed my uncle and joined the Air Force, naïvely signing a contract for the electronics field. That meant the Air Force could place me in any electronics job where I was needed, as long as I was qualified for the position. Unfortunately, I failed to obtain all of the facts and details regarding what the "needs of the Air Force" actually meant.

Whether or not the Marine was lying I will never know, but I am one hundred percent sure the Air Force recruiter lied. At boot camp I told the career counselor what my recruiter said about becoming a firefighter. Sergeant Pick-a-Job Now said, "Son, you've been screwed. Pick a job."

You may recall from a previous chapter when I discussed the dream sheet, and that day was my first introduction to the infamous piece of paper. Bear in mind this was the military, I was in boot camp, and there wasn't time to research jobs and ponder my future in the Air Force. Also, based on my aptitude test scores, there were only a limited number of career fields available for me to choose from. So I picked five jobs that sounded like good ones, and I didn't become a firefighter. Instead I ended up in a career field I hated: aerospace photographic systems repairman. At first it sounded like a job that would suffice until I became a firefighter, but I only grew angrier at my circumstances.

After graduating from boot camp in the late summer of 1976, I went to war. Those of you familiar with history are probably asking *what war?* The Vietnam War had ended, we weren't fighting any skirmishes around the planet, and we were not engaged in combat with the Soviet Union or the Martians. So what war? *This* conflict was only known to a small group of people. The war was Rick Davis versus the United States Air Force. This battle was not being waged between two nations, but rather by a short, angry guy from South Jersey who decided to take on one of the largest military organizations in the world. I was determined to become a firefighter in the Air Force and I did not care how the goal was accomplished.

Zig Ziglar said, "Motivation is the fuel necessary to keep the human engine running."[21] In order for your car engine to work there has to be fuel in the tank. Plus there needs to be an absence of mechanical problems. Sometimes people need to use starter fluid to get the engine running. However, that product contains highly volatile ether, and if not properly used, it may ignite in your face with a bang. So let's equate motivation to gasoline, and anger to ether. In my war with the Air Force, I added ether to my motivation more than once, resulting in a large bang of stupid decisions leading to poor actions on my part. During that time, there was an administrative captain in my squadron who was in a position to make life miserable for me because of my bad decision-making. Fortunately he understood enough about human behavior that he was sympathetic and willing to help me become a firefighter in the Air Force. His name was Captain Lemier, and I am grateful for his help. However, my underlying anger still simmered below the surface, waiting for something to ignite the fuel.

My pattern of irritation continued for several years. I brought the anger into my marriage. Although I never directed the anger at my wife, it certainly negatively impacted her feelings. There were times when our oldest daughter felt my wrath when I yelled at her. Although I never physically lashed out at my wife or daughters, I later learned how my anger created an atmosphere of tension and fear in the home. Even though I learned many lessons through this experience, I am not proud of this time in my life. I'm thankful for a godly wife who demonstrated patience and prayed for me on a daily basis to change.

THE TURNING POINT

In 2001, our family faced an extremely difficult situation. The stress began to register on my internal seismograph, sending signals that some impending disaster was about to happen. Finally, on a Sunday afternoon in February 2002, the eruption occurred.

I was on duty that day, and my engine was dispatched to a medical incident less than a mile from the fire station. Arriving on scene at the same time as the ambulance, we found a large male lying on the floor of his small trailer house, unconscious and barely breathing. At the time, our department still relied on a response from volunteer firefighters to assist, and none were coming to help us. This contributed to an increased level of frustration on my part, which did not help the situation at hand. I asked dispatch to send another notification for the volunteers and then requested a second fire department unit be dispatched for help. The paramedic was having a difficult time inserting a breathing tube in the patient's airway. I grabbed hold of the unconscious patient's belt on both sides of his body. Straining because of his size, I lifted him from the floor to straighten his airway so the tube could be inserted. The patient was clearly in distress and the four of us were stretched to our limits trying to keep him alive. All the while my frustration levels continued to rise.

Before the second fire unit arrived on scene, the door opened and one of our volunteer fire chiefs came inside. Instead of giving him direction on how he could help, I shot off my mouth in anger and said, "Another fine volunteer response!" Between the two paramedics, the five of us from the fire department, and a sheriff's deputy, we struggled in the cramped space to load the patient on the cot, remove him from the small trailer, and load him into the ambulance for transport to the hospital. The medics asked for one of us to drive the ambulance and also for someone to help attend to the patient. Seething in anger and determined to make a statement, I made an incredibly stupid decision.

The second unit dispatched to the emergency was the one and only ladder truck operated by the fire department. If I had opted for me and my driver to go to the hospital, we could have left our engine parked next to the trailer house and then found a ride back afterward. That would have taken only one unit out of service. Instead I chose to drive the ambulance and ordered the officer on the ladder truck to assist the paramedics in the back of the ambulance. Now instead of one piece of fire apparatus being out of service, my decision had taken two out of service, including the one and only ladder truck we had. The choice I made greatly impacted the level of service that Loveland Fire Rescue provided to the community.

Fortunately, there were no other emergencies during that time. After returning from the hospital we went to Fire Station 1, where I vented my anger and frustration regarding the previous emergency to my battalion chief—in front of several other firefighters. This particular incident occurred during a time in our organization's history when there was a remarkable amount of friction between the paid and volunteer staff. Under the influence of the stress of organizational friction while trying to save the life of a dying man, coupled with the circumstances my family was dealing with, and fueled by my ongoing anger, I erupted into a volcano of verbal rage and irresponsible decision-making.

We cannot choose the consequences that accompany our behavior. I knew I had allowed my emotions to control me. I knew I was wrong in getting angry like I did. I knew I was incorrect by taking two rigs out of service. I knew I was out of line by venting and fuming at my battalion chief in front of others. Yet, in some crazy, self-deluded sense, I was hoping it would just go away and be forgotten.

Two days later I was called into a meeting with our fire chief Mark Miller, the division chief, and my battalion chief. I will always remember that day as a pivotal, life-changing one. A little over four years had passed since being told by a previous shift commander that he knew who I was and what I was about. But instead of shooting my mouth off in a weak attempt at defense like I did in January 1998, I sat there helpless, awaiting the fate about to befall me.

The fire chief informed me that the volunteer firefighter I was belligerent with the previous Sunday had called to complain about my conduct. In a feeble effort to deflect the judgment of the court, I told the fire chief I would call the volunteer and apologize. The chief said, "I know you will, Rick. You always do. The problem is that you keep throwing rocks through the glass, we replace it, and then you throw more rocks. It's like the window behind you: there is a large pile of rocks there and something has to be done." I thought the chief was either going to fire me or demote me. I began to tear up, and it was not a false, emotional appeal to his mercy. I was a broken man who could no longer make excuses for his anger.

At that exact moment, God took hold of my heart and changed me in a way I did not think possible. Even though my life had been transformed in September of 1981 when I accepted Jesus Christ as my Savior, I still clung to the anger that had accumulated and multiplied through the years. On that day in February 2002, I was in the furnace, and impurities were being refined from my life. It is amazing what flashes through your mind at a time like that. Fear, humiliation, thoughts of having to look for another job, the need to pay the mortgage . . . all in mere seconds. If the chief wasn't going to fire or demote me, I expected he would order me to attend an anger management class. So I asked him if he would allow me to seek help from the pastor of my church, and he agreed. The chief also said I would be held accountable, and he required me to meet monthly with my battalion chief to document progress. I wasn't being fired or demoted.

The meeting was a humbling and painful experience, but needed and long overdue in my life. God's instrument for change in my life was Mark Miller, and I am thankful he grabbed the bull by the horns. Also, one of the lessons I learned during this meeting is this: leadership knows when to extend grace and mercy.

SEEKING HELP

After returning to our fire station, I called my wife, Debbie, and told her what happened during the meeting. She was grateful the fire chief confronted me and was thankful God was working in my life to change the pattern of anger. The following day, I called our pastor, Ward Smith, told him what occurred, and asked for his help. Ward said he had a little booklet to use and we would have our first meeting the following Sunday after church. When we met, I had no idea what to expect, but I knew I needed help and that I was going to be held accountable. Ward presented me with a small, thin booklet titled *Moses: His Anger and What It Cost Him.*[22]

I had read about Moses in the Book of Exodus many times, not to mention watching Charlton Heston portray him in the

1956 movie *The Ten Commandments.* Now that I had been confronted about my anger, the life of Moses and his struggle with the same problem took on an entirely different perspective. Additionally, I gained a greater understanding of how my anger adversely impacted those around me, including my family. I learned a simmering state of anger is a sign and symptom of discontent, associated with a lack of joy in our lives. I discovered that anger is a cousin to fear. Fear that I cannot control the future or everything in life. I also began to realize that anger was driving people away from me.

Furthermore, I recognized that angry leaders are ineffective leaders.

CONTROLLING ANGER

Do I still get angry? Of course I do; I'm human. But I've learned to rely on God to help control my responses. Ephesians 4:26-27 reads, "Be angry, and do not sin: do not let the sun go down on your wrath, nor give place to the devil." Anger is an emotion God endowed upon us and it's not the anger that is sin, it is how we react to it. For example, I get angry about crime and injustice. However, rather than form a group of vigilantes and take matters into my own hands, I must rely on law enforcement and the criminal justice system to address those issues.

What does it take to trigger your anger? Is it the person tailgating you in traffic or is it the loud party next door? Does it happen when you are tired and hungry? Do you get mad when a subordinate has been told to do something, but the job does not get finished? Maybe it's the employee who wants to know why something has to be done in a particular manner. Perhaps you don't like to be questioned and you expect unwavering obedience from the troops.

There are at least a hundred other scenarios that can make us mad, but how do we react in these situations? I knew a man several years ago named Explosive Eddie who drove a tractor-trailer delivering gasoline and diesel fuel to local gas stations. When Explosive Eddie saw people doing something he felt wasn't safe, he angrily confronted them. Now granted, when you're driving a truck with nine thousand gallons of flammable liquid on board, you certainly want the guy who is ten feet away to put out his cigarette before a fire starts. However, our approach to the situation impacts how the other person reacts. For example, if Explosive Eddie had said, "Sir, would you mind putting out your cigarette? This gasoline is extremely flammable and if there's a fire it might kill both of us." Most likely the guy with the cigarette wouldn't want to die in a fiery flash of flames and he would put it out. However, Explosive Eddie typically approached the situation by saying, "Hey, you stupid jerk! Whatta ya tryin' to do!? Kill us!? Huh!?" How would you react to someone yelling at you like that? Explosive Eddie often told me about the times when he yelled at his boss or chewed him out. Eddie was actually stunned when I expressed my amazement that his boss let Eddie get away with his behavior. Guess what happened—Explosive Eddie's boss finally got tired of the tirades, and fired him.

THE UNDESIRABLE CONSEQUENCES OF ANGER

Remember what I wrote earlier: we all make choices in life but rarely, if ever, do we get to choose the consequences. Sooner or later we will pay for our angry outbursts and behavior. Previously I described what happened after being confronted by the fire chief because of my anger. Eventually the monthly meetings with my battalion chief ended after he and the chief were satisfied with the progress I made.

The following year in July 2003, our department conducted testing for the position of battalion chief. The process involved a written test, an oral presentation, a tabletop tactical exercise in front of a group of fire chiefs, and two separate interview panels. I was one of three finalists for the position but I was not promoted. Why? The fire chief, division chief, and my battalion chief all told me I was qualified for the position and they knew I could do it. However, not enough time had passed for me to show them I had truly obtained a victory over my anger. Although that was a hard and bitter pill to swallow, I understood their position. The good news is the next time I tested for battalion chief in 2005, I was promoted to the position.

Another consequence of anger is the impact on your health. Medical problems may show up in a multitude of areas, such as the cardiovascular, nervous, digestive, or immune systems. There is also an increased risk of hypertension, heart attack, stroke, and gastric ulcers.[23] In the end, we have to ask ourselves if getting angry and blowing up like a volcano is really worth it? James 1:19-20 reads: "So then, my beloved brethren, let every man be swift to hear, slow to speak, slow to wrath; for the wrath of man does not produce the righteousness of God."

Anger drives people away from us and they are reluctant to approach a mad leader because of unpredictable behavior. One such example occurred prior to my promotion to battalion chief, when I worked as a lieutenant at our main fire station. I often took phone calls from firefighters at the other stations asking me what kind of mood the battalion chief was in. In essence, when I answered the phone, I functioned as one of two flags seen at the shore during hurricane season: one indicating a tropical storm warning and the other a hurricane warning.

I guarantee if you are cutting, berating, and yelling at your people, they will clam up and be extremely reluctant to say anything to you. Your anger is driving a wedge between you and your subordinates. Eventually they will not only distrust you, but they will avoid you at all costs.

Anger negatively impacts us physically, spiritually, emotionally, and mentally. Every day wrath continues to destroy marriages, friendships, working relationships, opportunities for advancement, and so many other enjoyable aspects of life. Do not become that person. If this *is* you, there is still time to correct your behavior. There is no way you can be an effective spouse, parent, friend, or leader if anger rules over you. We would do well to heed the words of Thomas Jefferson when he said, "Nothing gives one person so much advantage over another as to remain always cool and unruffled under all circumstances."[24]

Practical Application

- Leaders must exercise self-control over emotions. Proverbs 16:32: "He who is slow to anger is better than the mighty, And he who rules his spirit than he who takes a city."
- Never forget that uncontrolled anger leads to poor decision-making. Proverbs 14:17 states, "A quick-tempered man acts foolishly . . ."
- Don't make excuses for your behavior or fall into the trap of "That's just the way I am."
- Remember that life is full of choices, but rarely can we choose the consequences.
- Experienced leaders know when to extend the hand of grace and mercy.
- If you struggle with anger, seek out sound advice and help. A good source is Louie Giglio's book and online Bible study, *Goliath Must Fall: Winning the Battle Against Your Giants*.[25]
- Understand the negative impact of anger on your health, family, friends, coworkers, employees, and your career.

Watch Your Toes

New Jersey is known as the Garden State, and I still believe some of the best-tasting fruit and vegetables come from the many farms that dot the landscape. Driving past any of the vegetable stands at small farms during the growing season reveals cars with license plates not only from Jersey, but Pennsylvania, Delaware, Maryland, and New York. I've always been amazed that even though Jersey is the brunt of many jokes, people flock to the state to purchase vegetables, stroll along the boardwalks, and enjoy the seashore.

In the summer between my junior and senior years of high school I worked on one of the larger farms in Cumberland County. Joe, the landowner, had stopped farming and leased the property to a man named Lou, who raised Chinese vegetables such as bok choy, mustard, and horseradish. Each morning, my coworkers and I laid irrigation pipes in the fields, completed general cleanup duties, and built wooden crates for the vegetables to be packed in. We delivered the completed crates to the fields so other workers could fill them with the freshly cut vegetables.

After lunch we returned to the fields to load the packed vegetable crates on the trailers. One guy drove the tractor, one was on the trailer to stack the crates, and two walked alongside, lifting and heaving the heavy boxes onto the trailer. Fortunately, we took turns at each task, including the most coveted position, driving the tractor. The work was hard, hot, dirty, and sweaty—especially in the humid, sticky air of South Jersey. After a trailer was loaded, we drove it to a waiting area, took a short break, and repeated the same procedure several times until all the vegetable crates were retrieved from the field for the day.

Twice a week, we loaded crates into the back of an older Ford pickup truck. Those vegetables were destined for a Chinese restaurant in Philadelphia, and Lou always made the deliveries. Monday through Friday we also stacked vegetable crates into the back of a forty-foot tractor-trailer independently owned by two men from Alabama. They were nice guys, but I chuckled because both resembled pictures I had seen of Confederate soldiers from the Civil War. Sometimes I imagined both had marched twenty-five miles in the heat and humidity wearing wool uniforms, carrying heavy packs and muskets. Instead of driving an old International cab-over truck, they looked as if they were ready to storm the side of Little Round Top in Gettysburg. After we packed their truck full of vegetable crates, they delivered the produce to Hunt's Point in the Bronx section of New York City.

One afternoon, both Joe and Lou were present as we loaded the forty-foot trailer. Both of them grew impatient with us because they thought we weren't working fast enough. Instead of growing vegetables, Joe grew angrier with us as the minutes passed. He told us to get out of the way because he and Lou could do a better job.

Lou climbed into the seat of the red 1960s International Farmall tractor, and Joe started guiding him toward the back of the trailer. Joe's left hand rested on the front hood of the tractor as if he were steering it toward the intended target. It quickly became apparent that Lou was going to drive over Joe's toes with the right front tires of the tractor. Our boss, Harry, warned Joe, who curtly responded, "Mind your own business!" Acutely aware of the potential for injury, Harry sounded the second warning and was greeted with another angry answer from Joe. Undaunted, Harry sounded the third and final warning, but Joe would have nothing to do with it. After being told three times to shut up, Harry said nothing more and watched the unfolding show.

Although none of us were psychics, we all predicted the outcome. Sure enough! Lou inched the tractor forward. Slowly but surely the right front tire of the old red tractor contacted the toes on Joe's left foot and rolled over all five of the digits. Joe started shouting in pain "Oohh! Oohh! Oohh!"

I was reminded of a scene from an old *Three Stooges* movie, when Larry and Curly would do something stupid to hurt Moe. Lou finally stopped the forward progression of the tractor and sat there with a stupid, blank look on his face. In the *Three Stooges* movies, Curly would have said, "I tried to think and nothing happened."

Joe hopped around in pain while the four of us did what came naturally—we laughed at both of them until our sides hurt. Once the painful comedy show ended, Joe and Lou departed the area and left the work to those of us who knew what to do and how to do it.

Ah, yes. Frustration leads to anger, contributing to more anger, and ultimately painful consequences. Proverbs 22:15 states, "Foolishness is bound up in the heart of a child . . ." In this particular case Joe and Lou were bound up with foolishness. Joe limped away with a bruised ego and toes. No doubt Lou was glad it wasn't his toes throbbing in pain.

7 *Why Did You Do It?* The Positives and Negatives of Determination

"And let us not grow weary while doing good, for in due season we shall reap if we do not lose heart."

— Galatians 6:9

The thesaurus lists many synonyms for determination: willpower, resolve, tenacity, and perseverance. Although these words are looked upon as desirable character traits, those same qualities may create problems for the leader and the led. Just as every battery has a positive and a negative terminal, so does determination.

Thomas Edison's dogged persistence to invent the lightbulb is an example of a positive application of determination. In spite of numerous setbacks and disappointments encountered along the way, Edison continued to work on the project until it came to fruition. He could have easily given up, but he didn't. As a result, we do not have to light our houses and streets with gas lamps or candles. Claudio Fernández-Aráoz describes that type of drive as "the wherewithal to fight for difficult goals despite challenges and to bounce back from adversity."[26]

My brother Ron served in the U.S. Coast Guard (USCG) at Station Chatham on Cape Cod, Massachusetts, in the 1980s. This is the station written about in *The Finest Hours*[27] and also portrayed in the movie with the same title. Offshore are the shifting shoals of the Chatham Bar, the site of numerous maritime incidents throughout the years. During one Nor'easter while he served with the USCG, Ron witnessed an example of determination gone horribly wrong.

Nor'easters always bring high winds and surf, creating extremely dangerous conditions for anyone on the water. During the storm, Ron was part of a boat crew tasked with flagging down and stopping boats before they attempted to cross the shoals. At some point during the day, a small vessel approached the Chatham Bar with two men aboard. Following their orders to protect life and property, the USCG crew sounded the siren and used the loudspeaker to warn the men of the danger ahead. As the other boat slowed, Ron said it was obvious the two men aboard were discussing the matter. Suddenly their engine roared to life, and the small craft thrust toward the open and rough waters of the Atlantic Ocean. Their determination to leave the safety of the harbor led to a bad decision that day. Their boat capsized in the storm, and while it was recovered, the bodies were lost at sea.

As leaders, we must recognize when determination leaves the path of usefulness and turns detrimental to ourselves. Likewise, we must observe patterns of behavior in our subordinates and know when and how to address an issue before it turns into a problem. It is imperative that we guide a subordinate's resolve into useful channels. We need to help them avoid self-destruction because of a headstrong approach.

WHAT FUELS DETERMINATION?

What drives a person to accomplish a goal? Is it a burning desire for recognition and notoriety? Is it for monetary gain? Is it simply for personal satisfaction? Or does the person feel a yearning deep within, a calling to pursue a particular career path? The answers to these questions are important because they establish the motivation behind an individual's actions.

The yearning desire to become a firefighter is part of my life story. Everyone has certain childhood memories etched into their mind and one of those is my first ride on a fire engine when I was three years old, on Memorial Day 1961. A year later, a large fire erupted in Fortescue, New Jersey, on the Delaware Bay. One of the main routes to Fortescue was past our house. When we heard the fire engines approaching, my dad quickly took me to the street and I watched in awe as they raced by with lights flashing and sirens blaring. I remember the firefighters standing on the back step of the trucks waving at us as they passed by. When we went back inside our house, my dad gave me his badge from his time as a volunteer firefighter in Mauricetown, New Jersey. I still have the badge. It has a place of honor in a display case next to badges I have worn throughout my career.

Even though while growing up I also had an interest in becoming an astronaut or a geologist, my underlying desire was to become a firefighter one way or the other. Paid or volunteer. For those not familiar with firefighters, my story is not that unusual. Over the years I have met many men and women who wanted to be a firefighter since they were little kids. Like myself, they too were determined to reach a career goal.

At a younger age, my determination to become a firefighter was driven by many things. The idea of working in an exciting and dangerous job. The attraction of large, shiny red fire engines, ladder trucks, and rescue trucks. The notion of riding on the back step of the fire engine while responding to a fire. Plus the knowledge that firefighters help other people in times of need.

As the years progressed, my desire was further reinforced when the television show *Emergency!* premiered on NBC in 1972. Every Saturday night, I religiously watched Johnny Gage and Roy DeSoto and the men of Engine 51. I was riveted to the TV set. With each episode, I became more and more convinced that my future was in firefighting.

When I found my dad lying dead on the floor from a heart attack, I dialed "0" for the operator and summoned an ambulance. I then ran to a neighbor's house to get help. In the 1970s, my hometown did not have an emergency medical service, so help came from the nearby Fairfield Township Fire Company No. 1. It seemed like an eternity before two volunteer firefighters arrived in a white Cadillac ambulance to provide medical care for my father. As they loaded his lifeless body into the back of the ambulance, I vowed to become a firefighter. One way or the other, I would work toward achieving that goal for my life.

In 1973, a New York City firefighter I never met named Dennis Smith helped solidify my career choice. He authored *Report from*

Engine Co. 82. I could not put the book down. To this day it is still one of the best, if not the best, books written on the life of a firefighter. Ten years had passed since standing in front of our house with my dad watching fire engines drive by on the way to a fire in Fortescue. But I knew beyond a shadow of a doubt that I wanted to be a paid firefighter.

I read any available material on firefighting. I also became a frequent visitor at the volunteer firehouse less than a quarter of a mile from where we lived. Although the firefighters may have initially wondered what I was doing there, no one turned me away. In February 1976, I became a rookie member of the Cedarville Fire Company No. 1 and in my mind, well on the way to realizing my dream.

I HAVE MET THE ENEMY AND HIS NAME IS RICK

In the chapter on anger, I described my Air Force experiences after the recruiter told me I could not enlist as a firefighter. Following graduation from the aerospace photographic system repairman school, my next duty station was Seymour Johnson Air Force Base in Goldsboro, North Carolina. As disappointment turned into frustration, my resolve to become a firefighter led me down paths of unwise behavior, including my declaration of war against the Air Force. I was determined to prove that this large, bureaucratic military machine was not properly using me in the right career field. Surely someone from my unit up to and including President Jimmy Carter would understand my plight. Why couldn't the Air Force see how valuable I would be as a firefighter and not a camera repairman? I was absolutely dumbfounded and mortified that I was the only one able to see this fact.

At Seymour Johnson, my job was to repair the highly reliable KB-25 gun camera mounted on the front instrument panel of the McDonnell Douglas F4-E Phantom II jet fighter. The camera recorded footage when the pilot fired the 20mm Gatling gun located in the nose of the aircraft. The mechanical dependability of the camera was great for the aircrew, those who reviewed the tapes, and the taxpayers. But those of us who worked on the cameras were underutilized and bored, and we coped with low morale.

In the late summer of 1977, the USAF Tactical Air Command developed a program called POMO: production-oriented maintenance organization. The overall goal was to increase the efficiency of aircraft repair and engage underutilized people like myself in other maintenance fields. Through the program, I was afforded the opportunity to work with people in the jet engine shop, hydraulics shop, and other maintenance fields. I enjoyed working on and around the F4-E and there was a tremendous amount of pride and patriotism in doing so. But it wasn't firefighting.

Goldsboro was an eight-hour drive from South Jersey, and I spent many long weekends and all of my leave time in Cedarville, still involved with the fire company. In October 1978, my long-held determination to become a firefighter in the Air Force hit the peak of frustration. I traveled to New Jersey for a long weekend and attended a training class hosted by Fairfield Township Fire Company No. 1, the same fire department that had provided care to my dad. I was a heavy drinker during those years, and once the training concluded, myself and several other firefighters went to a bar. Downing one beer after another, I amused my comrades with stories of woe and how I was a victim of the USAF machine. I was supposed to be on the road back to North Carolina late that afternoon, but instead I was drunk and not capable of driving a car.

That afternoon I made a stupid, alcohol-fueled decision I am not proud of. The actions I am about to describe displayed an incredible lack of integrity. But I share this story in hopes that other leaders will see there is a bad side to determination as well as a good side. Hopefully, you may gain greater insight into some of the actions and behaviors driving your subordinates. In 1978 I was convinced the United States Air Force had singled me out for some cruel form of punishment and couldn't care less about me. Seeing no progress in my quest to change career fields and wallowing in my sorrows, I went AWOL (absent without leave). Three days later, the squadron First Sergeant called my house and said that if I wasn't back to work that night, he would send the police for me. I had never been in that kind of trouble before and I did not want the police hauling me off. Realizing how stupid I was and ashamed of my behavior, I went back to work.

WHY DID YOU DO IT?

I reported for my assigned shift at midnight. When I walked through the door, my immediate supervisor and friends expressed disbelief over my actions. I knew I'd made a poor choice, and some form of punishment would follow.

Around 2:30 a.m., the First Sergeant showed up at the hangar in his uniform. I cannot recall his name, but he was a tall, slender man with a kind demeanor—and it came through early that morning. The first thing he asked was, "Davis, why did you do it?" He patiently sat there and listened to every word I said, and he never got angry with me.

When I finished, he said that other than me being extremely vocal about wanting to be a firefighter, I had not caused any trouble. I remember him asking, "So you went AWOL so you can be a firefighter?" I told him yes and apologized.

What drove my First Sergeant to get out of bed at 2:30 in the morning to speak with me? He easily could have waited until normal duty hours, but he didn't. He did it because he was a leader who cared for his people. He could have chewed me out, but he didn't. He could have taken an authoritarian approach to the situation, but he didn't. He spoke to me like a disappointed father would speak to a wayward son.

My reaction to his questioning and comments was not obstinate or mutinous. I was ashamed and embarrassed at my actions and I apologized. His last words that morning were, "You know there will be consequences."

JUDGE AND JURY

A week later I was called into the office of Captain Lemier, the squadron administrative officer whom I mentioned in the previous chapter. The squadron legal officer was with him. As I stood in the position of attention, the legal officer read my rights. That was unnerving, and fortunately something I never experienced again. I thought my dream of becoming a firefighter in the Air Force had been destroyed because of my stupid, drunken decision.

Then Captain Lemier read the charge against me of being absent without leave. He also said I was being punished under

Article 15 of the UCMJ, also known as non-judicial punishment (NJP). NJP is handled at the squadron or battalion level without a judge or jury. The penalties could be confinement to the barracks, extra duty, a monetary fine, demotion in rank, or any combination of the four.

Expecting the worst, I braced myself as the captain issued the sentence: two weeks' extra duty. Then to my surprise and utter amazement, he said the extra two weeks would be worked at the base fire department. He had gone above and beyond to arrange an 89-day temporary duty assignment (TDY) for me.

EXTRAORDINARY LEADERSHIP QUALITIES

I was grateful and appreciative of how the First Sergeant and Captain Lemier handled the matter. Both of those men could have taken the easy path, followed standard military procedures, and left it at that. Instead, they chose the hard road of transformation, and I was the subject.

Let's return to the early morning hours when the First Sergeant confronted me about going AWOL. During the conversation, I had told him that, overall, the military was a good experience for me and if firefighting were my career field, most likely I would consider making the Air Force a career. Those two men saw my determination to become a firefighter and rather than crush me, they took an opportunity to help me achieve a dream. They realized my being a firefighter would benefit the Air Force as well.

At the conclusion of the 89-day TDY, Lemier was instrumental in obtaining a second temporary assignment to the base fire department. That was no small feat because Air Force regulations were specific regarding circumstances surrounding special assignments. On top of that, permission for the extension had to be granted from Tactical Air Command (TAC) Headquarters at Langley Air Force Base in Virginia.

When the second temporary assignment expired, the captain went to bat for me again. He worked with the chain of command in my original squadron, the fire department, and TAC headquarters to secure a permanent assignment to the base fire department. I was told the transfer would remain in effect until one of two things took place: separation from the Air Force at the end of my enlistment or an official career change. Fortunately, the latter took place, and I went on to become a firefighter and remained in the Air Force for another three years.

You may wonder why I didn't make the Air Force a career. After all, didn't I obtain the goal I was shooting for? The answer is yes, but the needs of the military overruled my desires. Less than a year before my enlistment came to an end, I received orders directing me to return to my first career field, aerospace photographic systems repair, because of a manpower shortage. That time it was the deputy fire chief at Lowry Air Force Base in Denver, Colorado, who came to my aid. He and I went to the Consolidated Base Personnel Office and produced the paperwork proving I was guaranteed the slot as a firefighter. That saved my bacon then, but the sergeant in personnel said if I reenlisted, my next assignment would be back on the flight line working on cameras.

Since I was determined to remain a firefighter, my next step was to pursue a job as a civilian firefighter with the Air Force. Unlike my previous behavior, I followed all rules and regulations. By this time I had accepted Christ into my life, and God blessed me with the job I was seeking. Eventually my career as a firefighter extended to the Marine Corps and then to Loveland, Colorado.

Practical Application

- Willpower, resolve, tenacity, and perseverance are synonyms for determination. All are desirable qualities as long as they are controlled and properly administered.
- Just as water can be channeled for good use at a hydroelectric power plant, we too must direct determination for good use.
- Understanding the underlying motivations for an individual's determination assists with their development.
- As leaders we must learn to recognize when determination is detrimental to ourselves and those we lead.
- Drowning our sorrows in alcohol never solves anything and leads to bad decision-making!
- Like the First Sergeant in this chapter, leaders can be firm and mean business at the same time as showing kindness and listening to their subordinates.
- When someone makes a stupid decision, consider the entire person, including their work ethic, the reasoning behind the decision, and so on. Leaders *will* recognize when a person needs a course correction in their life.

Charge!

As I write this, it is Black Friday, and throughout the United States people are saying, "Charge it." Retail outlets accumulate thousands of dollars in sales while consumers amass thousands of dollars in debt. Early Thanksgiving morning, people anxiously tear open their local newspaper, not interested in the latest news and sports scores, but seeking colorful advertisements with the best bargains. Hordes of people shove the last forkfuls of turkey in their mouths and with gravy dripping from their lips, hurry off to the land of retail amazement. As the clock strikes midnight and Black Friday officially arrives, caffeinated consumers wander from store to store with the same determination exhibited by Sir Edmund Hillary when he scaled Mount Everest. Tragically, I fear too many people place more interest in purchasing the newest electronic gadget or gimmick than personal and spiritual development.

The word *charge* has also been used in a musical way throughout history. On the battlefield, flags, drums, whistles, and the bugle were used to communicate orders and rally the troops. Most people are familiar with the bugle call to charge. Even thinking of the sound evokes images of a weary and dusty nineteenth-century bugler mounted on a large steed. Pressing the brass instrument to his lips, he sounds the call. Suddenly a hundred cavalrymen draw sabers and spur their mounts forward. Ear-piercing yells accompany the thundering sound of horses' hooves on the ground and two determined foes clash on the field of battle. The sounding of the bugle and yelling *charge* sends an electrifying signal to everyone listening that something is happening *now*! The bugle call indicates a steadfast resolve to move forward, face the unknown, and overcome hardships and obstacles.

As we go through life, many times we have to sound *charge* and move forward. Such was the case with my higher education. Growing up, I was never a big fan of school, although my favorite subjects were history, geography, and earth science.

My dad wanted me to attend college, and even at a young age, I wrote to several universities requesting catalogs and information. I said nothing to my dad as I gradually became more absorbed with a career in firefighting and less interested in college, as I did not want to disappoint him. After his death, I lost all interest in college. During my time in both the Air Force and Marine Corps, I had sufficient opportunities to pursue an education. I squandered those chances, living under the mistaken notion that I didn't need a degree.

After nine years in two branches of the military, I was used to a regimented and disciplined routine. Returning to the civilian world, I had a difficult time adjusting. In the Marine Corps, I enjoyed knowing I was part of something bigger than me. In other words, my job and life had a purpose. My new civilian job was a drudgery and I felt worthless. I hated the job and hated going to work. My boss knew that, so we mutually parted ways and I began searching for another job.

Seeking help from a career management firm, I was greeted with, "Our clients possess a college degree and you don't." This particular company was established after World War II with the intent of helping veterans reenter the job market. Fortunately, their original mission played in my favor and they accepted me as a client because of my veteran status. Unfortunately, as I continued the search for employment, the common mantra was: "You don't have a college degree." Happily, God opened a door and after several months I found employment.

Having read the writing on the wall, my wife and I decided I needed to finish my education. A university in Denver offered a program specifically tailored for adult learners in situations like mine. Taking advantage of the opportunity, I sounded the order to *charge*, moved forward, and graduated with a BS degree in business administration. The bugle call for *charge* sounded again, and I completed a master's degree in Executive Fire Service Leadership. Two years later, the bugler sounded again and I moved onward into the National Fire Academy's Executive Fire Officer Program.

Nothing is wrong with being smart consumers and taking advantage of Black Friday deals as long as we aren't charging ourselves into more debt. However, when the bugle sounds *charge,* leaders must demonstrate the determination to advance and improve ourselves personally, professionally, and spiritually. Otherwise, how will we ever be able to help someone else?

8 *I'm Sorry to Tell You, But . . .* Disappointment

"Defeat is simply a signal to press onward."

— Helen Keller, Author and Activist

On Wednesday, November 1, 2017, over 54,000 baseball fans packed Dodger Stadium to watch the final game of the World Series between the Los Angeles Dodgers and the Houston Astros. It was a pleasant evening with the daytime high temperature recorded at 72 degrees Fahrenheit. Periodically the television cameras landed on someone famous, but mostly the crowd consisted of excited fans wearing the hats and shirts of their favorite team.

The Series was tied at three games apiece. At the top of the ninth inning, the Astros were leading 5–1 when Dodgers pitcher Alex Wood took the mound. No doubt the Dodgers hoped to score runs and win the game when it would be their turn to bat at the bottom of the inning. Wood finished the inning with two strikeouts and a line drive caught in center field. The score remained 5–1.

As the Dodgers came to bat, the television cameras panned the dugouts from both teams and the crowd. I watched to see their facial expressions and body language. The Astros fans were filled with anticipation that their team was going to win. The Dodgers fans had expressions ranging from hope their team would pull ahead to dejection that they had lost the World Series. The Astros dugout was alive with excitement. On the opposite side of the field, the players in the Dodgers dugout anxiously waited to see what would happen. If they scored four runs it would tie the game and give them another chance. What if they scored five runs? Game 7 would end with the Dodgers winning.

The first Dodger at-bat was Chase Utley, who struck out swinging. The emotions of players and fans intensified. Chris Taylor stepped to the plate, but he grounded out to second base. Again, the reactions of players and fans were easily recognizable. Many of the Astros in the dugout resembled racehorses waiting for the gate to burst open. On the other side of the ballfield, the look of gloom and despair registered on the faces of many of the Dodgers. Corey Seager stepped to the plate for Los Angeles—he was the last chance for the Dodgers to stay alive in the Series. Charlie Morton delivered the pitch and Seager swung at the ball. Crack! Seager's bat contacted the ball and he sped toward first base. Unfortunately for the Dodgers and their fans, the season ended when Seager grounded out to second base.

The Astros dugout emptied onto the field and all the players converged on the pitcher's mound. There was a jubilant celebration with grins from ear to ear. Players were jumping in the air, piling on top of each other, hooting, hollering, and reveling in their win. Then the camera switched to the dugout for the Dodgers. Most of the players had left for the locker room, but some remained. They weren't celebrating. Their faces showed signs of defeat, disbelief, and sorrow. The 2017 baseball season was over.

Disappointment. Sometimes arriving in small doses and at other times tearing through our lives like a Kansas tornado. Unfortunately, this topic is rarely discussed or even mentioned in leadership classes, books, or articles. How we view, react to, and recover from the experience varies from person to person. It is important to remember that disappointment is a universal emotion. Not only for the leader but also for those we lead. We must understand the connection between expectations and disappointment. When hopes are high, there is a greater chance that letdowns will have a deeper impact.

FOUNDATION FOR EXCITEMENT OR DISAPPOINTMENT

Becoming a firefighter is a competitive, daunting task involving a series of stressful tests. Although the entry-level requirements vary from jurisdiction to jurisdiction, certain components are standard, such as the written test. My organization utilizes a third-party testing service measuring reading comprehension, mathematical ability, mechanical aptitude, and a human relations component. Additionally, the applicants must pass a rigorous physical agility test. All of this in hopes of being invited to an interview. If applicants score high enough in the first interview they will move on to a panel of chief officers for another round of questioning.

Depending on the size and needs of a fire department, there may be only one position available. But two facts remain: there are always more candidates than available positions and there will always be more disappointed people than happy ones. Many of those who weren't offered a job will find their names on an eligibility list. However, there is no guarantee anyone will be hired during the life of the list, which typically lasts six months or a year. That means when the eligibility list expires, the applicant must start the process all over again. If you ask a firefighter about their hiring experience, you will discover many of them endured the process several times before securing a job. These are the firefighters who persevered in the face of repeated disappointment.

But the process does not stop when Joe Schmuckatelli hears, "Congratulations! You made it and we are offering you a job." That is a *conditional* job offer and contingent on whether or not Joe passes a medical examination and background check. After Doctor Death determines Joe is healthy and not suffering from a chronic toe fungus, everyone awaits the findings of the background investigation. Finally Joe receives word that he has a clean record and there are no problems. He moves on and is happy. However, at times the doctor may find a serious, disqualifying medical condition in candidates, thereby eliminating them from further consideration. Once again, the ugly head of disappointment rears up.

In this example, Joe passes with flying colors and begins attending fire academy for three months or longer. The rookie firefighters are immersed in academic studies, daily aerobic and strength exercises, and strenuous physical activity involving such tasks as pulling hose, raising ladders, rescuing victims, and so on.

Periodically, a recruit is dismissed from the academy for reasons ranging from academic or physical failure, or behavioral problems. Disappointment. Some will start the application process again while others move on to a different line of work.

Buyer beware! Your new employee at Electrifying Energy may be the former firefighter who failed the academy and saw their dreams dashed on the rocks. As the leader you may play an integral role in helping that person successfully recover from their bad experience.

Finally, graduation day from the fire academy arrives. Joe is one of many firefighters standing in front of family, friends, and peers. They all gleam with pride as the fire chief pins the hard-earned badges on their chests. Within days each one of them reports to their newly assigned fire station to begin a one-year probationary period involving more study and more training.

Eventually, Firefighter Schmuckatelli looks to the future and desires to rise through the ranks. It may come as a surprise, but the fire chief doesn't walk into a station, point at Joe and say, "You're now a lieutenant!" Promotions in public safety agencies are generally earned through a rigorous and stressful testing process. This equates to more study, preparation, testing, and interviews for a limited number of positions. Those who are promoted experience happiness, joy, elation, and a sense of relief that the process is finished. For those who didn't get promoted, it means disappointment at being passed over. Many of them will try a second time, third time, or more before being promoted. Others stop the pursuit altogether. Some in the latter category may become bitter.

I have experienced both sides of the coin. Jubilant and excited when the fire chief called and said I was hired, and experiencing the same emotions later in my career when I was promoted. Also, disappointed and depressed after being rejected for a promotion. It's a story similar to the World Series described earlier. On one side of the ballfield, the Houston Astros were jumping up and down and piling on top of one another. They were ecstatic with joy and happiness. On the other side, the Los Angeles Dodgers were down and dejected. A fantastic contrast of emotions ranging along the entire scale from delight to sorrow. How hard we hit the ground is directly related to our degree of expectation and how much we prepare.

HITTING THE GROUND

Through early adulthood, the thought of continuing my education was not on the radar. Consequently I failed to take advantage of opportunities the military offered to obtain a college degree. After separating from the Marine Corps, reality struck home when I discovered that many employers would not speak to me because I didn't have a degree. Disappointment upon disappointment led to frustration, as my expectations were crushed. Returning to the fire service, I buckled down and obtained a degree in business management. Looking to the future and having a desire to be a chief officer, I earned a master's degree. Three years after promoting to the rank of battalion chief, I was accepted into the National Fire Academy's Executive Fire Officer Program. At that point in life my thoughts and preparation were directed toward the next level of chief officer positions, and my expectations were high.

The opportunity came in 2013 when I became one of three finalists for a division chief of operations job in a neighboring department. The process involved a telephone interview, tour of the department with the fire chief and a battalion chief (in other words, another interview), a candidate meet-and-greet with the fire department, followed the next day by four separate interview panels. I felt good about the process and anxiously awaited a phone call to learn whether or not I had the job.

When the call came, the fire chief said, "I'm sorry to tell you, but you didn't get the job." Wow! It hit me like three tons of bricks. Deep disappointment wasn't the only emotion that surfaced. Rejection, disbelief, failure, frustration, and other assorted feelings. My expectations plummeted to earth like a meteor.

But wait, there's more. Two weeks before the final interviews in the neighboring department, a vacancy occurred in my own department for a division chief of operations position. I believe strongly in maintaining integrity and I decided it would not be appropriate to withdraw from one process to enter another. Following the rejection phone call from the neighboring fire chief, I phoned my chief to let him know what happened. I also told him I would pursue the vacancy in our department. The interview took place two weeks later and it was between me and one other battalion chief. Approximately three hours after my interview, the phone rang and the fire chief said, "I'm sorry to tell you, Rick, but you didn't get the job."

THE EMOTIONAL STORM OF DISAPPOINTMENT

Bam! Two rejections for the same type of position, and within two weeks of each other. My emotional meter pegged in the red zone. I felt like an abject failure and questioned what was wrong with me. What would the men and women on my shift think? Would they even have confidence in my abilities to lead them anymore? Would they look at me as a failure? Would I be written off by the department as being inconsequential and unimportant? After all, I worked hard pursuing two degrees and was a graduate of the National Fire Academy's Executive Fire Officer Program. My sights were set on the division chief position and suddenly within the space of two weeks, my hopes crashed like the Titanic hitting the iceberg in the North Atlantic. I failed to recognize where I was emotionally, but my wife knew what was going on. I was depressed.

Fortunately, the men and women on my shift were extremely supportive. Other people didn't know what to say or how to act around me, and a few kept their distance. I don't believe it was malicious, just awkwardness of not knowing how to handle the situation. To compound my problems, four months later I found myself in the hospital suffering from acute kidney failure and diagnosed with cancer. But that is another story in itself.

HANDLING DISAPPOINTMENT

Happily, I am blessed with a loving, faithful wife who prays for me. I have two daughters who love and support me as well. Many people prayed for me during my time of extreme disappointment. A friend gave me the book *Why You Can't Be Anything You Want to Be* by Arthur Miller. It discusses our God-given gifts and talents, and how to seek God's plan for our lives. The intent is to allow God to transform our lives, and in turn, impact those around us. In Romans 12:1-2 the Apostle Paul wrote, "I beseech you therefore, brethren, by the mercies of God, that you present your bodies a living sacrifice, holy, acceptable to God, which is your reasonable service. And do not be conformed to this world, but be transformed by the renewing of your mind, that you may prove what is that good and acceptable and perfect will of God."

The oft-repeated adage that time heals all wounds should be taken with a grain of salt. What are the depths of the wounds, and how much time will be required for healing? That all depends on the circumstances and the person involved.

My experience was a gradual, up-and-down process, including many conversations with people helping me through the hard times. It also involved a continual reminder of 1 Peter 5:8, "Be sober, be vigilant; because your adversary the devil walks about like a roaring lion, seeking whom he may devour." Satan did not want me to have joy in the Lord. He wanted to keep me down and devour me. Eventually I realized God's plans were not my plans, and He had me in the right place and the right position.

Earlier I wrote that how we individually view, react to, and recover from disappointment varies from person to person. Although I have quickly bounced back from many disappointing experiences, that wasn't the case with the division chief positions because of the expectations I had built. More time was required to overcome that disappointment, but God and my family helped me rebound. People often say there is a reason for everything, and that is certainly the case for those who believe in Jesus Christ. Romans 8:28, "And we know that all things work together for good to those who love God, to those who are the called according to His purpose."

BENEFITING FROM THE STORMS OF DISAPPOINTMENT

Not only was I faced with a choice of how to respond to personal and professional disappointment, but I also had a choice of what to do with the lessons learned. One option was to bottle them up and never say anything for fear of resurrecting unpleasant memories. I could also choose to ignore the bad experiences and close my life to others in an attempt to demonstrate that I am a tough, stoic individual who can weather any storm. No good is accomplished by closing down our lives and shutting people out. Part of being an effective leader is to share our good *and bad* experiences with people. Otherwise, how will they learn? Leaders must take advantage of disagreeable experiences to help other people through their trials.

Always remember that leadership is not confined to the workplace. It has no boundaries. Unfortunately, far too many people in positions of authority don't share their personal disappointments; either that or they never experienced any that were serious. Consequently when someone they lead walks the path of disappointment, it is too easy for them to dismiss the struggles the other person is experiencing. Do you make comments such as: *Toughen up, that's the way the ball rolls*, or *Don't worry, there will be a next time*? Do you roll your eyes or shrug your shoulders? If so, you not only lack understanding, but you have a tremendous absence of compassion as well. I believe the majority of people are looking for their leaders to understand, demonstrate support, and provide meaningful encouragement. Some people describe this quality as emotional intelligence.

By the way, if you tell someone "I know how you feel" when they discern or suspect you haven't experienced major disappointments, you diminish your credibility. It will also anger them. Recently an individual shared with me that after being passed over for promotion, one of his bosses said exactly that. The person I was speaking with said, "He doesn't know how I feel because he's never been there! He's always gotten everything on the first try and he has no clue what it is like to be passed over!"

If you were hired on your first attempt, or promoted the first time you tested, be careful how you frame your statements to the person who did not receive a position. Instead of "I know how you feel," a better statement is, "I imagine you are experiencing some great disappointment about this." Taking that approach opens the door for a meaningful conversation and provides more opportunities to help them prepare for the next time.

Through experience, I learned the best approach is a short, succinct contact with the person. If possible I prefer to do this face to face. Otherwise I make a phone call. "Hi Bill. I heard that you didn't get the position and I'm sorry. Is there anything I can do right now?" Bill will appreciate the personal contact, he will remember it, and you are building a connection with him. Let Bill express his feelings and vent frustration, but in a respectful manner. Listen to him but don't make the mistake of rushing to offer solutions or a plan for the future. Stephen Covey said, "Seek first to understand, then to be understood."[28] Tell Bill you will schedule a time within the next two to three weeks to discuss the situation and develop a plan for the future.

As a leader, if you have dealt with major disappointments, you have the opportunity to create shared experiences with the other person. You may be asked how you felt and how you handled it. The individual may also want to know what you did to prepare for the next opportunity. The list of questions is endless, and so are the prospects of helping that person.

You should also understand this process takes time. Are you truly willing to invest in the life of that person? If so, you are a leader. If you don't want to take the time, then you are a leader in name only.

RESILIENCE OR RESENTMENT

Resilient people have the ability to weather the storms of life, learn from their experiences, and move on to the next challenge. They accept the fact that life is like an iron furnace where people are forged into stronger, more productive individuals. Yes, there will be more disappointments, but these are the people better equipped to handle them. They are the ones who grow and become stronger leaders. Usually this is a small group, and we need to groom them for higher levels of responsibility.

Many people also allow life's disappointments to create bitterness and resentment. At times they seem to thrive on these negative feelings, bestowing upon themselves a victim status. As with so many other areas in life, this is an individual choice. We can choose to be resilient or we can choose to be bitter.

Hebrews 12:15 says, "Looking carefully lest anyone fall short of the grace of God; lest any root of bitterness springing up cause trouble, and by this many become defiled." When reading that verse I often think of the invasive bindweed plant. Left unattended it takes over gardens and yards, weaving through fences and wrapping around vegetables, plants, and trees. Pulling the bindweed from the ground exposes long roots. That is exactly what happens when bitterness takes root in our lives. Failing to address the problem allows the roots to grow deeper into the emotional crevices of life. Eventually the bindweed of bitterness and resentment chokes the happiness and joy out of a person's life. As leaders we must protect against the bindweed, both in our own lives and with those we lead.

ADDRESSING DISAPPOINTMENT AT WORK

I've talked about disappointment from the employment standpoint of hiring and promotions. However, leaders must realize that hurt and disappointment associated with damaged or destroyed relationships, health issues, death, and a thousand other circumstances are real. When a subordinate faces a personal crisis, the problem comes to work with them.

The notion of leaving difficulties at the door or in the locker room is nothing more than a fallacy. Leaders who adopt that line of thinking are deliberately avoiding the issue at hand. It is not uncommon to see decreased work performance, attention-to-detail issues, and even behavior issues with employees who are going through trying times. The men and women on my shift are human beings. If someone on the shift experiences a personal problem away from work and I approach the issue the same way I would as a mechanical breakdown on the fire engine, then I am failing as a leader.

Far too many leaders treat personnel matters as if the people were pieces of machinery. As a matter of fact, leaders in that category would rather handle a mechanical breakdown than an emotional crisis with a subordinate. Multiple reasons exist why someone avoids these problems. The supervisor may be unwilling to say something because they dread the confrontation, or fear the employee will tell them to stay out of their personal lives. I am not suggesting you appoint yourself as an untrained counselor and provide advice beyond your capabilities. However, when personal complications enter the workplace and impact performance, the leader has an obligation to address the matter. Yet another reason why leaders must know organizational policies and the resources available to help employees during times of need.

Practical Application

- Disappointment is a universal emotion for both the leaders and the led.
- Disappointment is linked to our expectations. The higher the expectation the greater the chance of disappointment.
- Communicate how the disappointments in your life helped create perseverance and resilience. Romans 5:3-4, "And not only that, but we also glory in tribulations, knowing that tribulation produces perseverance; and perseverance, character; and character, hope."
- Subordinates respect leaders who have shared experiences.
- When addressing disappointment with others, avoid using the cop-out clichés such as *buck up, toughen up, saddle up, I know how you feel,* etc. Do not treat people like a piece of machinery.
- Remain alert to the invasive bindweed of bitterness.
- Remember the chapter-opening quote from Helen Keller: "Defeat is simply a signal to press onward."

An Overwhelming Desire

Our yearnings may be the size of a small cardboard box, or they may grow to the proportions of a Beverly Hills mansion. Sometimes individual cravings lead to addictions and a life of crime. A junkie hooked on methamphetamine may stoop to robbing liquor stores to support a life-destroying habit. The need to constantly experience a high and escape reality is an ever-present force in their life.

Menacing cravings also lurk in the depths of our bodies . . . strong urges accompanied by gurgling and growling sounds emanating from below. An urgent message traveling more than twenty inches from the stomach to the brain imploringly asks for relief. Instead of an encoded SOS (send out someone), the stomach repeatedly asks for SOAP (send out another pie). Not apple, pecan, coconut custard, or any other standard pie, but the ultimate pie. The prize of life. Pizza pie!

Growing up in New Jersey, I developed a deep love for good, quality pizza. To this day I still consider the delicacy as one of the basic food groups. Some may find this hard to believe, but the military did not serve pizza in the mess hall during boot camp. I'm sure there was a mistake or oversight on the part of some general in the Pentagon who did not understand the motivational qualities associated with such fine food. Another astonishing fact is no one asked if we wanted pizza. We simply stood shoulder to shoulder and sidestepped through the line while the cooks plopped something resembling food on our plates.

I knew boot camp would not be a cakewalk, but I had no idea of the hardship associated without my beloved pizza. After being cruelly deprived of the delicacy for what seemed an eternity, I experienced deep pangs for the culinary delight. The year was 1976 and the Air Force sent me to Lowry Air Force Base in Denver, Colorado, for advanced training. As far as I was concerned, Denver was the western frontier. I was surprised to see actual city buses operated by RTD (Regional Transportation District) and not stagecoaches from Wells

Fargo. I learned the Pony Express had ceased delivering mail years before and the U.S. Postal Service assumed those duties. Other modern amenities existed such as telephones, television sets, automobiles, Sears and Roebuck stores, and even fast-food restaurants.

Bolstered at these amazing findings, my expectations grew. Perhaps there was a glimmer of hope on the horizon. In the darkness, my eyes strained for the faint red light of a neon sign flashing "Pizza by the slice." With salivating taste buds and a gurgling stomach, I launched on a quest to find treasure. The sign at the base bowling alley advertised pizza and I ordered a slice. Bleh! Just as the stormy waves crash against the rocks, my hopes were dashed. My taste buds were aggressively assaulted by a piece of balsa wood drenched in ketchup with some cheese on top. Oh, the humanity of it all! In desperation I searched the Yellow Pages for a pizza establishment close to the base. Without a car, I would need to walk to a pizza joint or take the RTD bus.

At last I learned of one local company delivering pie to the base. The owner of the now-defunct Pizza Czar had developed a unique concept for delivering their food. The restaurant made one size of pizzas, but offered different toppings. The cost of a cheese pizza was five dollars, and one with meat was priced slightly more. Even though the Pizza Czar delivered to the base, you didn't call them on the phone. We stood in front of the barracks and waited for the truck to arrive. The vehicle was an early 1970s burnt-orange Chevy Step-Van with an orange flashing light on top. When the driver ran out of pizza, he turned the light off and went back to the shop for more food. The business owner obviously knew it was good business to sell mass-produced food to hungry military personnel on the base.

Desiring pizza and with no other way to satisfy my cravings, I ventured to the street in front of the barracks. Scanning the horizon and searching for the distant flashing orange light, I anxiously awaited the arrival of the truck with a five-dollar bill in my hand. The Chevy finally appeared and the orange light was still flashing. I was in luck! Pizza! I exchanged my money for the hot, flat box that was already stained with grease on the bottom. Returning to my room, I opened the lid and there it was: a nice, greasy cheese pizza. I imagined the slices curling up as if beckoning me to bite into the tasty dish.

In the midst of devouring the first slice, my taste buds rebelled. Suddenly there was a revolution taking place between my hunger pangs, my deep desires for good pizza, and my taste buds. As I continued to shove one piece after another into my mouth, my brain overloaded. Finally gaining control, I arrived at the painful realization that the Pizza Czar defrauded me. What lay before me was not the flavorful pizza pies I had come to love in New Jersey. This was a piece of cardboard, smeared with something akin to stewed tomatoes, and sprinkled with cheese. I was the victim of naïve thinking. I honestly believed pizza everywhere tasted like the pizza I grew up with. My expectations were obliterated like an atomic blast.

Fortunately for me, the long-awaited moment my stomach craved finally arrived. At Christmas in 1976, I traveled back to New Jersey and made my way to Big John's in Bridgeton. Walking into the shop, I was greeted by a multitude of pleasant aromas. The deep red sauce, basil, fennel seeds, sausage, pepperoni, and the smell of the ovens. At last my needs to consume a fantastic pizza were realized. Each of us experiences overwhelming desires and expectations, and it does not take much for the pendulum to swing. Our expectations may produce feelings of elation and happiness or they may swing to disillusionment and piercing disappointment. As leaders, we need to know how to address this swing in ourselves and with our subordinates.

9 | *Embrace the Chaos* **Decision-Making**

"A good solution applied with vigor now is better than a perfect solution applied ten minutes later."

— General George S. Patton, Jr., U.S. Army

Making decisions in a timely and effective manner is a critical component of leadership. Your reputation as a leader and the confidence people have in you are influenced by the decisions you make.

As a fire department battalion chief, I face a multitude of decisions on a daily basis. Every shift, I must adjust the staffing roster to accommodate vacations, illnesses, injuries, or special-duty assignments. I make those decisions in the confines of an office and generally time is on my side. On the opposite end of that scale are the decisions I make as an incident commander. A structure fire doubles in size every seventeen seconds, consuming the contents and building until firefighters stop the forward progress of the flames. A wind-driven wildland fire burning uphill in dry grass, brush, and timber rapidly advances across the terrain. In both situations, time is not on my side, and the fires will not wait for me to make decisions.

My interest in the study of decision-making began on a cool, overcast afternoon in October of 2006. That day Captain Mike Cerovski, who was the department training officer, and I conducted training evolutions for my shift using a device referred to as the "Christmas tree." The "tree" consists of a vertical pipe approximately ten feet tall. Several horizontal pipe branches with small holes are attached to the vertical piece—thereby presenting the appearance of a tree. The device is plumbed to a large thousand-gallon propane tank and the flow of gas is remotely controlled by valves. There is also a valve at the base of the tree for the leader of the hose team to turn off once the crew reaches the fire.

One of the main objectives of a drill involving fire is to assess the company officer's ability to size-up (evaluate) the incident, and develop an initial incident action plan (IAP). The IAP is based on what the officer observes, what actions are being initiated, and what resources are needed. In any fire the objective is to locate, confine, control, and extinguish the fire. Additional responsibilities include search and rescue, ventilation (creating an opening for heat and smoke to escape), protecting property, and overhaul (searching for hidden fire). In other words, the company officer is tasked with making quick decisions in a stressful, chaotic environment. For this particular drill the location of the fire was obvious and there were no needs for search and rescue, ventilation, salvage, or overhaul. However, all the other elements of the size-up and IAP were still necessary.

The training officer slowly opened the valve to the Christmas tree and the white propane vapor began flowing from the holes. I approached the device wearing the appropriate personal protective equipment and a self-contained breathing apparatus (SCBA). Walking toward the hissing sound of escaping propane, I held a lit torch attached by a hose to a twenty-pound propane cylinder. Propane is heavier than air, and I waved the torch back and forth along the ground until the vapor cloud ignited. Captain Cerovski increased the pressure of the escaping gas and the fire roared to life, sounding like a small jet engine.

Meanwhile, the three engine companies involved in the drill waited at the entrance to our training facility. Keying the microphone on the radio, I dispatched the companies to a reported propane tank on fire threatening structures at 710 South Railroad Avenue. Mike fully opened the gas valve and the flames intensified.

In less than a minute the first engine company arrived and the lieutenant provided a brief size-up over the radio stating what he observed, what he was doing, and what he needed. A hose was stretched from the engine and laid out on the ground, but it was not charged with water. Time appeared to stand still as the crew of the first engine engaged in a discussion. I surmised they were trying to decide what to do next. I called for the second engine to respond, and Mike and I anticipated the officer on that rig would take command of the situation. Nothing happened with the two crews except more discussion. I radioed for the third engine to respond, fully expecting action on their part. The crew stepped off the engine, walked over to the other two crews, and joined the discussion. Mike said, "Rick, I need to lower the pressure because we're wasting propane."

That is when I decided to take action. I approached the group and told them someone had better make a decision and put the fire out. Now! The hoses filled with water and a lieutenant took charge of the crews. He formed two teams of firefighters and under the protection of a fog stream (wide-angle water stream that resembles a curtain), they pushed the fire back until the valve at the bottom of the Christmas tree was exposed. The lieutenant reached down, turned the gas off, the fire was extinguished, and the crew backed out to their original positions.

Upon conclusion of the drill, we gathered around and conducted an after-action review (AAR). One objective of an AAR is to identify strengths and weaknesses. The incident action plan is discussed and compared to what actually happened. What went well, what didn't go well, and why—for both the incident action plan and the real-time event. Finally, what needs to happen in order to sustain strong areas and/or improve weak ones?

Personal attacks are not permitted, but accountability is expected from each individual. Our AAR revealed the reason the first arriving officer did not take command. He was simply following the new direction established by the fire chief, who had said he did not want the first officer taking command of an incident. The second arriving officer did not take command due to the uncertainty of what was actually taking place. The third arriving officer did not take command either. He made the assumption that the second officer had established command based on the direction of the fire chief.

The AAR exposed uncertainty, confusion, and disorder among the crews. Everyone was exasperated. There wasn't any *disintegration* of command because no one had *taken* command. Why? Because the fire chief's directive to the department deviated from long-standing, established local and national practices. In the absence of leadership, decisiveness vaporized, indecision ruled, and no action occurred.

Every person at the drill knew what to do. All of them were veteran firefighters and good at their jobs. It was not a question of incompetence or lack of understanding. Furthermore, I never doubted their knowledge, skills, or abilities. The drill did not go well due to an absence of decision-making. However, in the end, the training exercise was a success because everyone learned from the difficulties.

From the time I had taken command of the shift, I encouraged people to think out of the box. I assumed everyone understood what the phrase meant, and the same words were repeated during the AAR after the drill. One of the lessons *I* learned that day was to never presume people understand what I say.

Part of my job as a battalion chief is to teach and mentor, so I uttered the words, "Hey guys, you need to think out of the box!" All of a sudden, from out of the small crowd gathered around the back of a shiny red fire engine, I heard a captain ask, "What in the world do you mean by thinking out of the box? You say it all the time and I don't know what you're talking about." I was stunned. More than two years had elapsed since I took over the shift and he had never asked what I meant until that afternoon.

His question brought a two-fold problem to light. The first one was my assumption people understood what I was saying. Regardless of how often an expression is bantered about by us or society, not everyone knows what it means, and not everyone will ask what it means. The second problem was the captain waited until we had a less than stellar drill to ask what the phrase meant. Aha! The learning moments in life.

Here's a bit of irony. During peaks of solar storm activity, people worry about interferences to communications systems around the globe. Yet we don't attach the same importance to disruptions in daily face-to-face communication. Miscommunication and misunderstandings impact decision-making, and sometimes, the consequences can be serious. Later in the chapter, I will address the impacts of decision-making.

THE BRAIN AND DECISION-MAKING

The outcome of the after-action review launched me on a path of research and discovery, asking the question, *How do people and organizations make decisions?* In 2007, I read an article in the *Harvard Business Review* by David J. Snowden and Mary E. Boone titled "A Leader's Framework for Decision Making."[29] They described four environments where decisions take place: simple, complicated, complex, and chaotic. I thought to myself, "Chaotic!? Hey, that's our world of fire and rescue."

Many times, we are dispatched to emergencies with little information beyond an address, and sometimes that isn't even correct. Arriving on scene, we are often met by excited people yelling that it took us thirty minutes to get there and we need to do something. After the Gettysburg Campaign in 1863, Major General George G. Meade wrote his wife and said, "The most difficult part of my work is acting without correct information on which to predicate actions."[30]

I continued researching the topic and began teaching classes on decision-making to my shift. After one class, I had a discussion with a lieutenant who expressed frustration with some of the situations we face at the scene of an emergency. I replied, "Hey! Embrace the chaos! We respond to emergencies in a world of uncertainty and disorder."

Although I had read a number of resources on decision-making, it wasn't until 2009 when I learned much more on the subject. In September of that year, I embarked on the four-year Executive Fire Officer Program at the National Fire Academy (NFA) in Emmitsburg, Maryland. The program targets senior fire officers and provides courses in Executive Development, Community Risk Reduction, Executive Analysis of Fire Service Operations in Emergency Management, and Executive Leadership. The NFA recently restructured the program, but when I attended, the length of each course was two weeks on campus. After each class I had six months to successfully complete an applied research project (ARP) before returning the following year. Plus, successful completion of the fourth-year ARP was required before graduating from the program.

My first ARP was *Making Rapid Tactical Decisions Under Stress*. The research determined factors contributing to stressful decision-making and how to improve the decision-making process.[31] My second ARP related to the topic was *Situational Awareness at the Command Level*.[32] The information gleaned from both research projects revealed how the brain works when decisions are made. The research also laid bare how little I knew about the subject and how much more there is to learn.

We make decisions multiple times every day, most of them unconsciously or with little thought. When Joe Schmuckatelli takes the elevator to the top floor of the Sears Tower in Chicago, he doesn't stare at the buttons and wonder what to do. In less than a second, Joe looks at, selects, and pushes the appropriate button to take him to the desired floor. On the return trip he pushes the button with the arrow pointing down. The door opens, Joe steps into the elevator and pushes the button marked "G" for ground. Next thing he hears is *ding*! The door opens and Mr. Schmuckatelli is at street level and off to purchase a famous Chicago-style Italian sandwich. Providing the elevator didn't get stuck between floors, it was a simple decision-making process.

Other decisions require more time, thought, and prayer, such as marriage, careers, options for medical treatment, and significant financial matters. Situations like these allow us time to weigh the pros and cons and consider the potential outcomes. On the opposite end of the spectrum are high-stress professions requiring rapid, critical decision-making while operating under extreme pressure.

You may be thinking, "Rick, I don't fly planes, fight fires, arrest people, or perform surgery. So how does this business of rapid decision-making impact me?" If you operate a motor vehicle on any street or highway, inevitably you will make split-second decisions to avoid other vehicles, pedestrians, or objects in the roadway. If your two-year-old niece is running toward the rain-swollen drainage ditch, then you are going to make a quick decision to stop her. Every person walking the face of the earth encounters situations necessitating fast decision-making.

My research revealed the following influences which impact our ability to make decisions:

- Our physical and mental state
  - Are you tired, hungry, or sick?
  - Is your attitude positive or negative? Are you courageous or afraid?
- Training, education, and experience levels
  - Does one area outweigh the others?
  - Will these three components help or hinder you?
- Knowledge, skills, and abilities
  - How confident are you?
  - Do you recognize your limitations?
- Circumstances and the surrounding environment
  - Are there threats to your health, safety, employment, finances, etc.?
  - Is the decision environment quiet and serene or chaotic and confusing?
- Existing information
  - What do you know about the situation and circumstances?
  - How accurate is the information?
- Pressure of the unknown
  - Do you function well under stress?
  - Will your situation get better or worse?
- Available time
  - Is there an immediate need to decide?
  - Is time your friend or enemy?
- Criticality of the decision
  - Who is impacted by your decision?
  - What is impacted by your decision?

- Situation awareness
  - What is your level of discernment and understanding of the circumstances?
  - Can you anticipate what will happen next?

CAST OF DECISION-MAKING CHARACTERS

Decisive people are competent and overcome fear. Their confidence is displayed in a characteristic referred to as "command presence." Leaders with command presence remain calm, cool, and collected regardless of the situation unfolding around them. These individuals have their act together. They are professional and move about in a methodical, controlled manner with a tempo matching the situation. For example, there is a marked difference in tempo when a firefighter changes a smoke detector battery compared to providing CPR (cardiopulmonary resuscitation) for a person in cardiac arrest.

On the other side of the coin are the people who can't make a decision to save their own lives. Indecision results from numerous issues, such as incompetence, fear, lack of experience, and the absence of confidence. I've drawn from my personal experience and created composites (with fictitious names) which you might recognize. Do you know any of these people?

Calm Chris: Quality training, years of experience, professional knowledge, and job skills enhance our ability to perform the task at hand without losing control. In turn, those qualities bring a calming effect to the people around us—this is command presence. The individual who displays this is Calm Chris. On June 12, 2000, an illegal campfire west of Loveland ignited the Bobcat Gulch Fire, ultimately burning 10,599 acres of grass, brush, and timber. Approximately five hundred structures were threatened during the fire. Unfortunately, twenty-two buildings and several vehicles were burned. I was a lieutenant working on an engine company but not assigned to the first day of the fire. The following day I was assigned to the incident. Later that afternoon the fire blew up, producing a classic, towering column of smoke. Due to the dangers involved, everyone was pulled off the fire line and sent to their safety zones.

While we waited for orders and watched the smoke column tower into the air, I monitored our main radio frequency. Engine 3 was dispatched to a grass fire in an area called Masonville, less than five air miles from our location. We wondered if Engine 3 was being sent to a new fire, a spot fire originating from the main body of the Bobcat Gulch Fire, or to assist people concerned about the Bobcat Gulch Fire?

Calm Chris was the lieutenant on Engine 3. He's now retired, but was known for his firefighting skills and ability to remain calm under pressure. Our answer came when he radioed dispatch and said, "Notify the Sheriff that we need to evacuate Masonville." His radio report indicated the Bobcat Gulch Fire jumped into a nearby valley, threatening the entire ridgeline northwest of that location. Chris's radio report was so calm you would have thought he just ordered a cheeseburger in the drive-through at a fast-food restaurant. He displayed a professional command presence that is inherent with people who handle stress well.

Whirlwind Willy: Then we have Whirlwind Willy, whose eyes are dilated so wide they look like frying pans. He bounces around in an excited state like a steel ball inside a pinball machine, his voice steadily rising to a crescendo. Willy acts like he was struck with a cattle prod and his language is a cross between Russian and Chinese. No one has any clue what he wants. Others who are prone to such behavior are immediately influenced by the unknown dialect. Now *their* ability to make safe and sane decisions plummets to earth like a lead balloon.

I dealt with an individual such as this on a wildland fire in another part of Colorado. I was in charge of a strike team consisting of five fire engines from various departments, including Loveland. Our assignment was to protect structures threatened by a fast-moving, wind-driven fire. After driving from the staging area to our designated location, we waited for our division supervisor to receive further orders. Suddenly a smaller emergency vehicle came down the road. I thought, "Who is this?" The person jumped out, ran toward us, and started issuing orders in an excited manner. It was the operations chief for the incident. He shouted orders that made no tactical sense whatsoever, then said, "Wait! I'll be right back!" We watched him drive up the road approximately two hundred yards. Then his truck stopped, turned around, and he came back to our location. Pointing to a small group of houses, Whirlwind shouted, "Take your rigs up the road and protect those structures!"

I didn't say it, but I thought, "No fooling, Sherlock! That's what we were told to begin with." He left and we never saw him or our division supervisor the rest of the night. Our mission was successfully completed without Whirlwind Willy, and we were relieved at 6 a.m. the following morning.

Absent Ava: Whirlwind Willy's cousin is Absent Ava. The division supervisor in the previous example was physically absent, but Ava is mentally absent. This person is marked by paralysis and gripped with fear. Staring aimlessly into space, her mouth is wide open, resembling the Holland Tunnel connecting New Jersey with New York City. Individuals like this are oblivious to anything happening around them. You could steal her wallet and car keys at the same time and Absent Ava would never know it. This individual is powerless and incapable of making a decision. Consequently, Ava's authority is abdicated to subordinates who will make a decision for her.

During my first two years in the Air Force, I worked on the McDonnell Douglas F4-E Phantom II fighter jet. As a young man I naturally expected to have a supervisor who was technically proficient and competent with her job. Not so. My boss was Staff Sergeant Absent Ava and she woefully lacked those two qualities. She was also unable to make important decisions. Consequently, everyone else in the shop made the decisions for her. I do give Staff Sergeant Absent credit for knowing when it was time to make a fresh pot of coffee. However, she never decided to clean her filthy coffee cup until we tied a maintenance red tag around the handle that read DO NOT USE. Fortunately for the Air Force and the sake of national security, that person reached the maximum years of service for her rank and was discharged from the military.

Teddy Teeter-Totter: Absent Ava has a brother named Teddy Teeter-Totter. Teddy is the moderator of the mind-numbing, endless meeting where the same topic is repeatedly discussed without resolution. Mr. Teeter-Totter goes back and forth like a giant swing at an amusement park. Teddy believes time is on his side and lives by the philosophy that "Rome wasn't built in a day and neither was the Washington Monument." At the fast-food restaurant, he's the guy pondering whether or not to have American or pepper jack cheese on his burger. Mustard or ketchup. Pickle or relish. White bread or whole wheat. Waiting in the long line behind him, you're pushed to the point of yelling, "Come on, Pal! You ain't buyin' a car!" And the cycle repeats over and over throughout this individual's indecisive, inconclusive life. The King James Version of the Bible addresses this person in James 1:8: "A double minded man is unstable in all his ways."

Sally Socialite: Teddy's aunt is Sally Socialite. The majority of Sally's decisions center on whether or not she will gain or lose friends. Sally was one of my supervisors in the Marine Corps. She proved to be very successful as a recruiter and was even meritoriously promoted. In Sally's regular career field, her guiding light was based on how popular her decisions might be. She was smart and possessed the knowledge to effectively assist her subordinates through technical challenges. Yet she agonized over important decisions because she wanted to be everyone's friend.

Sly Stepping Stone: Sally's Godfather is Sly Stepping Stone. Sly is the most devious and deceptive person in the family. He bases his decisions on what makes him look good and what will help him get ahead of everyone else. Sly is adept at manipulating and controlling his boss by exhibiting extraordinary talent that no one else appears to have. Many of his subordinates are fooled by this façade and love working for him. Some possess the same distasteful qualities as Sly and they know his true character. Yet they use him and ride his coattails to promote their careers.

However, a few of Sly's subordinates and associates know who he really is and refuse to get caught in his web of duplicity. He quickly tosses aside his peers who know the truth. But woe to the poor subordinates who don't kiss his ring or sing his accolades. They find decisions not going in their favor. When Sly was young and inexperienced, those who weren't fooled by him saw how his decisions negatively impacted the truth seekers. But as Sly grew older and more experienced, his actions began to mirror a clever Ponzi scheme, often deceiving potential detractors.

Kaleidoscope Kelly: Finally, there's the drunk uncle in the family, Kaleidoscope Kelly. He has more than one, but rarely all, of the characteristics previously described. One moment Kaleidoscope is calm, collected, and devious. Two hours later he's running around like a chicken whose head was cut off. Later that night, you find him outside staring at the stars waiting for the mother ship to whisk him away to another planet. But in reality, he already is on another planet.

IMPACT OF DECISION-MAKING

You do not have to be a firefighter or member of the military to see or be one of these types of decision-makers. They have relatives in law enforcement, medicine, aviation, industry, food services, churches, and a thousand other places. Your ability to make decisions impacts everyone around you in one way or another.

Consider the descriptions of Whirlwind Willy, Absent Ava, Teddy Teeter-Totter, Sally Socialite, Sly Stepping Stone, and Kaleidoscope Kelly. I have worked for everyone on the list and know how they impact others. You must understand that your capacity to make decisions sends a strong message about your character. People *will* gauge your leadership and credibility based on this. How you make decisions impacts the morale of subordinates. Your capability to make decisions has bearing on whether or not people want to work with or for you. Your ability to make decisions will influence future assignments. Your decisions may influence the safety, health, and well-being of people. Your decisions may have significant sway over family, corporate, or organizational finances. Your decision-making skills affect the amount of trust placed in you by family, coworkers, superiors, customers, and the public.

Would you rather be one of the aforementioned characters, or a Calm Chris? His command presence builds confidence in subordinates. He performs well under stress and pressure. Dynamic and demanding situations do not rattle his cage. On September 11, 2001, President George W. Bush was visiting the Emma E. Booker

Elementary School in Sarasota, Florida. An aide whispered in his ear while he sat onstage, and told the President about the terrorist attacks against our nation in New York City, Washington, D.C., and Shanksville, Pennsylvania. President Bush's facial expression was solemn, stoic, and displayed concern. His lips were lightly pursed together as he listened intently to his aide. Yet he did not panic. He did not stand up and uncontrollably wave his arms in the air. He was concerned about how his reaction would be felt by the children in the room. There was incredible pressure on his shoulders to start making critical decisions relative to national security. However, he handled the moment professionally and with poise. Summed up, President Bush exhibited command presence. That is what I want in a leader and I suspect you do, too.

HOW TO MAKE BETTER DECISIONS

You can learn how to make better decisions, though it takes hard work and commitment. Education is a good start; however, it's not the end-all solution. Remember, there are a lot of people with college degrees sitting behind bars because they made unethical and illegal decisions. Learning how to make better decisions involves commitment, reading, and study. Books and articles about history and biographies are fantastic ways to learn. Also, review case studies to obtain insight on how others make decisions. I encourage you to place yourself in the shoes of the people you read about. Instead of condemning the person or group, ask: Why did they do it? What would I do in that situation or in a similar one?

You can also ask your supervisor to send you to professional classes, training, and seminars. Seek out and associate with people in your profession and other career fields who have a reputation as good decision-makers. Ask what factors they consider when weighing the evidence. Conduct your own after-action review and ask questions: What was planned, what went well, what didn't go well, and how can I or we improve?

Practical Application

- Heed the advice of General Patton: "A good solution applied with vigor now is better than a perfect solution applied ten minutes later." Do not become a zombie when it is time to make a decision.
- Do not assume everyone understands your direction. Ensure clarity.
- If you do not understand something your boss has been telling you, then ask for an explanation.
- Be aware of the factors impacting decision-making, such as physical and mental condition, availability of information, training, education, experience, etc.
- Dedicate the time to reading history, biographies, and case studies to learn how others make decisions.
- At times, decision-making is daunting and stressful. Prepare for those circumstances and face them with boldness and courage. Embrace the chaos!

I Should Have Known Better

I have a picture taped to my desk at the fire station. It's John Wayne portraying Marine Corps Sergeant John Stryker in the 1949 movie *Sands of Iwo Jima.* The quote at the bottom of the photograph reads, "Life's tough, but it's tougher if yer stupid." The picture has been in circulation for a number of years, and even though I've seen the movie more times than I can count, I don't recall John Wayne uttering those words. Nevertheless, I like the quote. Unfortunately, it has applied to me many times.

In early February 1980, a rare storm struck eastern North Carolina, blanketing Seymour Johnson Air Force Base in Goldsboro with twelve inches of snow. Places like Buffalo, New York, or Fairbanks, Alaska, are prepared for that much snow, but not Wayne County, North Carolina. I was on duty at the base fire department that Sunday and nearly everything had ground to a standstill—with the exception of our imaginations.

What could we do to fill our time during the snowstorm? One of our local adventure-seekers devised a plan to use a serving tray from the kitchen as a sled. We tied a piece of rope to the back of a four-wheel-drive fire department vehicle, and one by one, we took turns kneeling on the tray while the truck pulled and spun us around the large parking apron in front of the firehouse. The wind was blowing the snow and visibility was poor. However, the visibility was not poor enough to hide our antics from the personnel working in the air traffic control tower. No doubt they were jealous over our fun-filled winter adventures because someone in the tower called the assistant chief and told him what we were doing. In no uncertain terms, he ended our homemade bobsled competition. We should have known better. I should have known better.

Attached to the roof of the fire station at Seymour Johnson AFB was a small tower that at one time served as the alarm room, also known as the dispatch center for the base fire department. At some point prior to my working there, the Air Force had deemed the tower unsafe and condemned the structure. However, being young, daring, professional firefighters, we felt the warning did not apply to us. After all, we thought we needed to rappel and we thought the tower was a great place to descend from. On a warm, spring Saturday afternoon, four of us decided to become adventurous and go rappelling.

An interior ladder led from the alarm room to the top room of the tower. After climbing high above the station and enjoying the view, my friend Larry tied one end of a manila rope to a piece of metal and tossed the other end out the window. Each of us took turns securing ourselves to the rope and rappelling from the tower. Even though I doubted the wisdom of our activity, I still participated.

I had taken two turns when Larry said he wanted to do it once more. As we stood on the ground watching, the rope broke and Larry fell to the roof of the fire station. We scrambled to the top of a ladder previously placed to the roof, and found Larry sprawled on his back, deeply gasping. All the air had been knocked out of his lungs. Fortunately, he was not hurt, but we should have known better. I should have known better.

Twenty-three years later, I was working as a lieutenant on Engine 5 at Loveland Fire Rescue. On a beautiful, cloudless day in early July 2003, I decided to take my crew to a nearby lake for training. Our fire engine carried five hundred gallons of water in a tank. However, that does not last long in firefighting, so we must obtain water from a fire hydrant or another source, such as a lake or river. The latter operation is referred to as drafting. A large, hard hose, six inches in diameter, is attached to the side of the fire engine and the other end is placed in the water source. The driver primes the pump, a vacuum is created inside the pump, and atmospheric pressure pushes the water into the hose, thereby creating a continuous source of water for firefighting.

On the afternoon in question, my driver Janet parked the engine next to the lake and we prepared to start our training session. I cautioned her and the other person with us to be careful around the edge of the lake because the large rocks and concrete debris could easily injure them. I no sooner finished my warning when I stepped off the back of the fire engine and tumbled down the side into the rocks. Accompanying the fall was a loud pop in my right ankle, followed by pain and instantaneous swelling. Janet helped me out of the rocks and I called for an ambulance.

When our battalion chief showed up, he asked what happened. Janet told him I had made her mad and she had shoved me into the lake. Janet recently retired, but we had fun with that story up to her last day. Fortunately, I didn't break anything, but I did incur a bad sprain. However, I was placed on light duty for almost two months. I should have known better.

Many times I should know better, you should know better, and we should know better. I laugh at recalling each of these stories. We make good and bad decisions. Sometimes within seconds of making a choice we wish we had selected another path. In the end, if we can laugh at the decision and consequences, then we shouldn't take ourselves too seriously.

10 *Let's Get a Cup of Coffee* **A Wise Investment**

"Someone's sitting in the shade today because someone planted a tree a long time ago."

— Warren Buffett, Investor and Philanthropist

Are you taking the time to invest in the lives of other people? Are you planting and cultivating the seeds of growth in your employees, family, friends, and acquaintances? If you cannot answer yes to these questions, are you truly leading? One of the most important elements of leadership is developing others and encouraging them to grow personally, professionally, and spiritually in their own leadership endeavors.

Many years pass before a small seed grows into a mature tree. The coffee tree is no different; three to four years elapse before beans are produced. According to the National Coffee Association, "Not only does coffee power your day, it also helps power the U.S. economy."[33] Their market research revealed a $225.2 billion impact to the U.S. economy in 2015. Consumers spent $74.2 billion on coffee in the same year. In the United States alone, 1,694,710 people are employed because of the dark liquid drink. Based on these facts and figures, buying stock in the coffee industry could be a wise financial investment. Ultimately the monetary rewards may allow you to comfortably sit under a shady tree sipping a cup of coffee.

However, the topic of this chapter addresses something far more important: investing your time and money into the lives of other people. Sitting down with a small group or a one-on-one meeting over a cup of coffee reaps rewarding and long-lasting benefits. However, it takes more of your time to invest in people than it does to call your financial advisor to tell her you want to buy $1,000 worth of stock in Amalgamated Caffeine. By setting aside time to read this book, you are investing in your personal growth. Will you invest this new knowledge into the lives of those you influence, or will you allow it to fade away in your memory?

REASONS TO INVEST IN PEOPLE

I believe there is a responsibility to invest in the people I am accountable for, and those I come in contact with. This is based on Luke 12:48, ". . . For everyone to whom much is given, from him much will be required; and to whom much has been committed, of him they will ask the more."

Organizations fondly say people are their most important asset. If you believe that statement, prove it by developing the individuals working for you. In another chapter, I outlined the process of hiring and training an entry-level firefighter. The costs associated with recruiting, equipping, and training employees for any occupation count for a substantial financial investment. This doesn't include other expenses associated with promotional processes, conferences, guest speakers, internal training, etc. If organizations invest money into the aforementioned items, then why wouldn't we devote the time and money to develop our employees into better leaders? Not investing in people is foolishness.

When we take the time to develop people personally and professionally, everyone benefits: the employees, the organization, customers, family members, friends, and more. The results are productive staff members who enjoy coming to work. True, the possibility always exists of the employee leaving for another job, but we should not allow that to become a stumbling block in their growth.

On the flip side of leaders developing others are employers and managers who deliberately hinder the growth of their workers. Supervisors falling into this category often keep a thumb on people because they view their subordinates as threats. They are more interested in building a following than developing leaders. Every organization has at least one: the Pied Piper of Popularity.

Generally, they are skilled and adept in many areas, yet they are insecure enough to keep professional counselors employed for a lifetime. I've witnessed their approach to kingdom-building throughout my career, and it's nauseating. The Pied Piper of Popularity may see initial success with their approach, but eventually the smart people see through the façade and flee to the Kingdom of Truth. They seek leaders willing to invest time and effort into their lives. People want to be led by those who are secure and not threatened by subordinates. People want leaders who are skilled at bridging gaps.

LEADERS CONNECT WITH PEOPLE

Prior to 1926, people traveling between Philadelphia, Pennsylvania, and Camden, New Jersey, used ferry boats to cross the Delaware River. That year marked the opening of the Delaware River Port Authority Bridge, now known as the Benjamin Franklin Bridge. The structure spans 9,650 feet across the river.[34] Ninety-two years later, several bridges connect New Jersey with not only Pennsylvania but Delaware and New York as well.

The bridges improved economic and commercial relationships between the four states. They also allowed greater ease of travel, permitting families to visit relatives once separated by two major rivers: the Delaware and Hudson. Joining the two sides of the rivers involved money, material, labor, and *time*. Today thousands of people use the bridges on a daily basis for work, commerce, and leisure.

Likewise, to be a successful leader we must connect with people, and doing so means building relationships. There is no other way to positively impact and influence the lives of those you lead. The notion that leaders should be distant and aloof is a flawed philosophy. Detached leaders sprout disconnected employees who only comply because they have to, not because they want to. I have worked for both the connected and the distant leader, and more positive results came from the former.

We connect with other people by being genuine and creating an atmosphere where growth thrives. Demonstrate an interest in their lives, families, work, hobbies, and so on. This is easily accomplished by asking questions such as: *How's your family doing? What challenges are you facing at work? Do you have any plans for the long weekend? What are your goals in life?* Listen intently to what is being said and don't interrupt.

Be careful: do not ask questions just to give the impression that you care. People see through phoniness. I have experienced situations where supervisors are in a hurry and only feign interest in my life. I would rather have a boss be direct and get down to business rather than playing a game of "I don't really care for my employees, but I'm going to make them feel good by asking a few questions." That is either a self-centered manager who doesn't care for people or someone who is socially awkward. Whatever the case, that type of person is not leading.

The time I devote to the men and women on my shift takes many forms. It happens during station visits, semiannual performance evaluations, one-on-one meetings, crew members stopping by my office, training sessions, and even at the scene of emergencies. I realize that many reading this book do not work a twenty-four-hour shift, and finding time to spend with your subordinates may be extremely challenging. Nevertheless, you must find the time because personal contact is necessary to develop other people into successful employees and leaders.

Take advantage of opportunities when they arise and be prepared to provide answers. Recently my wife and I were in the business and leadership section of a bookstore. There was a younger lady in the same aisle who asked me, "Do you read a lot of business books?" I said mostly leadership and management books, along with military history. She then asked, "What do you think are the top three qualities a leader should have?"

Her questions turned into a forty-five-minute discussion on leadership. Clearly she was thirsty for knowledge and open to learning. I commended her for her desire to learn and for having the courage to address a complete stranger with the questions. In order to take advantage of opportunities like this, leaders must be friendly and open to others. The point is: take advantage of the opportunities God gives you to impact and develop other people regardless of who they are, where they live, or where they work.

QUICK DISCONNECT

On an opposite note, when you are speaking to Joe Schmuckatelli, do not walk away from him when someone of higher authority or perceived importance enters the room. That action is rude, demeaning, and a guaranteed path to disconnection with Joe. Being discourteous sends a clear message that he only matters when no one more important is around.

Unless someone walks into the room with their hair on fire or is having a heart attack, the individual you are speaking with at the time is the most important. If the other person is experiencing a true emergency, then Joe will understand when your attention is directed to another person's immediate need. However, if there isn't an emergency, Mr. Schmuckatelli knows what is happening when you walk away from him to speak to his highness King Arrogant of Egoville. Joe knows you are kissing the king's rear end, and you will have a difficult time getting any traction with Joe in the future. If you fall into that category, apologize to Joe and work at changing your behavior. Even at the young age of sixteen, George Washington penned Rule 1: "Every Action done in Company, ought to be with Some Sign of Respect, to those that are Present."[35]

Remember, leadership is about *people* and managing is about *things*. Leaders are visible and accessible. If your employees continually see you working behind the computer or locked in an office, then both parties will disconnect from each other. Eventually problems arise and people are unhappy and discontent. You may be thinking, "Easy for you to say, Rick! You don't know how much work I have and how little time there is." You're right. I don't know your situation, but I do know about establishing priorities.

WISELY TRIAGE YOUR TIME

Triage is a French word meaning "to sort" and is commonly used during rescue incidents involving large numbers of patients. Precedence is given to patients with life-threatening injuries. Patients with serious, but not life-threatening, injuries fall into the second priority, and the third category includes the walking wounded. Their injuries are minor and do not require immediate attention. The final group is composed of the dead or fatally injured.

In the fire service, we frequently respond to motor vehicle accidents involving multiple injuries. In order to sift through the chaos and properly allocate our resources, triage is of the utmost importance. The person screaming the loudest may not be the most critical. It's the quiet person with slow and labored respirations or profuse bleeding that often is the one dying. When triage isn't performed at the scene of a multi-casualty incident, the attention of firefighters and medics is easily misdirected away from the most critical patients.

Everyone you are responsible for requires attention in varying degrees. It is far too easy to direct your time and effort to the person screaming the loudest, and completely miss the one who wants your help, but may not ask. In another chapter, I addressed the blood-sucking vampires draining the life out of the leader. I'm not suggesting you put a toe tag on these people and identify them as being fatally wounded, therefore depriving them of your attention entirely. However, until you see a meaningful and substantial change in their lives, you have to guard your time with them. They are 3D people: disgruntled, dissatisfied, and disenchanted. Do not overlook the individual who appears to be sailing in smooth waters, as they need your time as well.

Leaders must prioritize their time when cultivating employees, family, friends, acquaintances, and others. Eliminating this step eventually leads to overload and your rubber band is stretched too thin. If you devote an inordinate amount of time to coaching, counseling, and mentoring, you *will* fall behind in other areas of your work. As a consequence, your health, productivity, and those around you suffer. I am reluctant to describe this as a balancing act because that implies attention in equal parts. A more accurate explanation is a juggling act. The leader must juggle all of their responsibilities with the obligation to develop subordinates. Professional jugglers learned the skill through hours of practice, patience, and desire. The person onstage juggling glass bottles didn't start with an object that would break so easily and potentially injure them. They began with objects easy to handle and worked up to the more difficult. Likewise, it takes time to learn triage and to juggle leadership responsibilities.

INVESTING YOUR TIME AND EFFORT

When you sit down with a cup of hot coffee, have you ever considered how much time and effort was involved before you took a sip? The coffee farmer nurtures the seed into a sapling. When the appropriate time arrives, the farmer plants the tree in the ground. Previously I said that three to four years pass before the coffee tree even produces beans. In the meantime, the farmer carefully raises and tends to the trees. Generally the crop is harvested only once a year, and many growers handpick the cherries containing the coffee bean. Then the process of drying, milling, sorting, and roasting takes place. All of this happens before your favorite coffee shop grinds the beans and brews a cup of java for your consumption. The time from planting the seed to brewing the beans spans several years.

Likewise, building relationships and developing others necessitates nurturing, cultivating, and an investment of time. The time required varies, depending on the circumstances and people involved. Each individual is unique, possessing a distinct personality, skill set, talents, and gifts. More than likely, they have interests and aspirations that differ from yours. There may also be differences in age, gender, education, and culture. Leaders work at bridging those gaps and not making them wider. Building relationships involves making connections between people; it does not always indicate fishing buddies or intimacy. Hallmarks of successful relationships are open communication and a desire to work with one another, whether or not you spend time together socially.

HONEST AND CONSTRUCTIVE FEEDBACK

Honest and constructive feedback is integral to developing people. We must understand that withholding beneficial advice hinders growth and development. However, far too many leaders have taken an unofficial oath of silence.

We live in a world where achievement ribbons are distributed like bottles of water. People wear their emotions on shirt sleeves and expect to be told all is well. Many employees expect to hear they are doing just as well if not better than the next person. As a result, too many supervisors live in fear that they will hurt feelings or offend subordinates if they tell the uncomfortable truth. Some individuals in positions of authority want to maintain friendships with coworkers, and they dread losing after-work camaraderie.

Some supervisors are gripped with the fear of confrontation or perceived confrontation and they never say anything negative to an employee's face. All too often, these same supervisors engage in the sneak attack. They mistakenly believe that inserting less than glowing comments in a written evaluation will avoid confrontation. But conflict breaks out when the employee is completely taken off guard. The supervisor is viewed as dishonest, untrustworthy, lacking integrity, and an overall coward for not previously saying anything. Proverbs 29:25 aptly states, "The fear of man brings a snare, But whoever trusts in the Lord shall be safe." Supervisors, bosses, and people in positions of authority who live in fear are not leading. They are also not contributing to the worthwhile development and growth of the people they are responsible for.

Genuine and useful feedback must also be specific. A common phrase for some years has been the hollow and overused cliché, "You rock" or "You're a rock star!" What does that mean? Are you being compared to a successful and talented singer such as Bruce Springsteen or Crazy Clyde's Wild Kazoo Band? Generalized, *ad nauseam* statements such as "You rock" mean nothing to many people. When a subordinate is doing a good job, be specific with your compliments. Say, "I appreciate your attention to detail. The information you provided in the report is not only accurate but is thorough and useful for the budget justification."

Watch and listen to the judges on any of the competition food shows on television. You will hear statements and descriptions like, "You achieved a level of difficulty with your dish that is indicative of a master chef. You superbly blended complex spices to create a dish that is not only aesthetically appealing but pleasing to the palate." Using detailed language sends a message to the recipient that their hard work and effort are appreciated. The employee also knows they are on the right track and doing the job correctly. Specific statements require more thought on the part of the leader, but the feedback is more beneficial and significant than empty phrases.

Failure to intelligently articulate practical, meaningful feedback inhibits the growth of the other person and reinforces bad habits and subpar performance. Bear in mind fluffy, misleading statements contribute to a subordinate's belief that all is well. For example, Dianna desires to climb the career ladder. She's worked for the organization for the past ten years and desires more responsibility and a higher salary. Yet Dianna is repeatedly passed over by individuals with less seniority and experience. She cannot get over the hump, and Dianna cannot figure out the reasons why.

What's going on in Dianna's life? A supervisor or other participants on the promotional interview panel are afraid to tell her the truth. They don't want to be viewed as bad people. They want to make Dianna feel good about herself. As far as Dianna is concerned, she is hanging her hat on accomplishments from ten years ago. She's been told, "You rock!"

Dianna hasn't been challenged to greater heights and she has not taken the initiative to improve herself. She's a mediocre employee and everyone knows it, including the boss. The supervisor is afraid to tell Dianna she could be producing better work and outcomes. An overwhelming fear pervades the workplace that Dianna will hire a lawyer.

There are supervisors (notice I did not use the word "leader") who choose the easy and less confrontational path of avoidance. They prefer to allow Dianna to walk through life in ignorance of the true problem rather than addressing the issues with her. Dianna slips into discouragement and bitterness over the process. Her complaining becomes more pronounced. Dianna believes a good ole' boy system is in place and she's not part of the favored group.

What happens when someone actually has the courage to tell Dianna the truth? It becomes evident her supervisor and so-called friends have lied to her. In the end little good has been accomplished for Dianna, the supervisor, or the organization.

Tell the truth and hold people accountable for their actions and development.

Organizational practices also inhibit the development of employees. During my career, I've sat on a number of promotional panels for other fire departments. On one occasion, the candidates were directed not to seek feedback from the evaluators. The third-party company conducting the testing process provided performance data to the participants based on a numerical system. However, numbers only tell a small part of the story, because it is impossible for a score to identify what areas a person needs to improve upon. Although some will say this is necessary to protect the organization, in the long run individual growth is stymied and ultimately the entire group suffers. In order for people to grow and develop, we need to hear more than "Your score ranked you slightly below average." The individual needs to hear why they are below average and why they did not receive a promotion.

Sidestepping difficult conversations regarding performance and development issues does not make your life easier. Avoidance begets avoidance, and in the long term, more harm is done than good. A breeding ground of frustration, bitterness, and indifference takes shape with the employee. Left unchecked, their poor attitude *will* spread to others and you will have an even greater problem to handle. Therefore, it is incumbent upon the leader to muster courage and develop people in both their good and difficult times.

Practical Application

- Leaders have a duty to develop others. Take time to plant and cultivate the seeds of growth in your employees, family, friends, and acquaintances.
- Remember, time is required for a seed to grow into a sapling and then a mature tree. Exercise patience and avoid creating unrealistic expectations.
- Development builds upon the financial investments spent on your employees through recruiting, hiring, and training, and contributes to retention.
- Leaders must connect with others and bridge gaps to build successful relationships.
- Perform developmental triage to define priorities.
- Provide honest, respectful, and constructive feedback through open communications.
- Mark Twain said, "What is the most rigorous law of our being? Growth. No smallest atom of our moral, mental, or physical structure can stand still a year. It grows—it must grow; nothing can prevent it."[36]

The Canoe

When I hear the word "canoe," several images come to mind. The calm, serene Bear Lake in Rocky Mountain National Park, Colorado, surrounded by snow-covered peaks. Two campers hoisting their canoe overhead to portage between lakes in Minnesota. The smell of cedar trees as the canoe glides through the waters of Cedar Creek in Cedarville, New Jersey. A fisherman in the middle of a small pond casting his line and hoping to catch a trout. A late-1960s, pale yellow Volkswagen Bug with a sixteen-foot piece of aluminum lashed to the top. Wait a minute! How does a VW Bug with a piece of aluminum on top figure into these images?

The answer lies in the person who owned the car and the canoe. His name was Cliff Sheppard, my uncle. His wife, Phyllis, was my dad's sister, and they lived in the house next to ours in Cedarville. Sometime during the '60s, Uncle Cliff purchased the canoe. He also developed a unique system to put the boat on top of his car by building two sawhorses the same height as the Bug. When he wanted to go canoeing, Uncle Cliff pulled the Bug alongside the sawhorses and easily slid the canoe onto a rack attached to the top of his car. I have vivid images of him pulling out of the driveway, shifting through the gears as he gained speed, all with this large piece of metal nearly dwarfing his vehicle. It was a hilarious sight, but Uncle Cliff loved to go canoeing.

He was a machinist by trade and a World War II veteran of the U.S. Army fighting in Europe. Like so many other veterans of the war, he rarely spoke of his time in the service. He would only tell me that he drove ammunition trucks and had three of them blown out from under him. After that type of excitement, it's easy to see why he wanted to own a canoe.

Each year, Uncle Cliff painstakingly planted a garden. He didn't own a gasoline-powered tilling machine to turn over the soil. His method involved pushing a hand plow through the dirt. Each weeknight in the spring and summer and on Saturdays, he meticulously weeded and watered the garden.

Gardening was not only a labor of love for him but a method of relaxation. He also raised pine trees on a small section of his property and I remember him periodically cutting one for Christmas. Growing up, my brother and I would often play in the "forest" next door to us. Uncle Cliff dumped used coffee grounds into the dirt around the trees. When he wanted to go fishing, he went to the tree farm with a shovel and dug up huge worms to use as bait.

One year he built a small brick structure to burn trash. Those were the days before the State of New Jersey banned open trash burning. Occasionally he placed a metal grate over the top of the structure and grilled hot dogs, often sharing with me. No doubt many are cringing at the idea of frankfurters cooking over a pile of trash. Remember, he survived three ammunition trucks being blown up beneath him, so any dangers associated with his cooking method were trivial compared to his time in the Army.

After the death of my dad, I spent quite a bit of time with Uncle Cliff, talking to him while he tended his garden or burned the trash. One day he asked if I wanted to go canoeing. We went to Menantico Ponds east of Millville, New Jersey, to canoe and fish. At lunch we went ashore on a small island covered with cedar trees and holly bushes. I love a good Italian sub and they taste the best when eaten outdoors. After Uncle Cliff and I finished our meal, we paddled to a more remote section of the pond. The calm, dark waters were carpeted with lily pads sprouting beautiful flowers.

One summer evening he took me to Union Lake in Millville. When we were in the middle of the large lake, he said, "I'm going to go swimming." Naively I thought we would return to shore to drop off the canoe first. Suddenly I felt the canoe shifting from side to side. Precariously balancing himself, Uncle Cliff removed his trousers to reveal the swimming trunks he was wearing. In a matter-of-fact manner, he stated it was easy to jump over the side without tipping the canoe. Sure enough, he dove over the side as the narrow piece of metal swung wildly back and forth. Not knowing how to swim and convinced I would die by drowning, I was fearful of what was going to happen when Uncle Cliff tried to get back in the boat. Amazingly, he successfully maneuvered his way back into the canoe and the Millville Fire Department did not have to respond to a water rescue incident.

Uncle Cliff died in 1989. I have fond memories of time spent with him in the garden, burning trash, and plying the waters of South Jersey in his canoe. I also have memories of a man who took his time to prevent me from doing something stupid I would later regret. After my dad died I had little interest in school. Desiring to become a firefighter, I felt the quickest path to accomplish my goal was through the military. I also thought an even faster route was by quitting high school. Uncle Cliff saw the foolishness of my plans, and one afternoon, he took off work. We went for a drive to Vineland, New Jersey, and visited the military recruiting offices. We started with the Air Force, followed by the Marines, and then the Navy. Pointing at me, he said to each recruiter, "He wants to quit high school and join the military." All three recruiters had the same response: "We won't take you until you finish high school." One of them added, "The Army will take you but they'll make you a cook." I was frustrated, angry, and disappointed at the recruiters and with Uncle Cliff.

During my junior year of high school, I settled down and saw the light at the end of the tunnel. The day after turning eighteen, I stood in the Armed Forces Entrance and Examination Station in Philadelphia and entered the delayed enlistment program for the Air Force. Six months later I graduated high school and went to boot camp. It wasn't until my senior year of high school when I realized what Uncle Cliff had done for me. He was a hard-working man and had taken time off from his job in an attempt to save me from dropping out of high school. Uncle Cliff had invested time and effort into the life of his nephew.

On my visits home from the military, I always made sure to go next door to see Aunt Phyllis and Uncle Cliff. Unfortunately, my wife and daughters never had the chance to meet my dad or Uncle Cliff, but I often speak of them. Earlier I described my uncle as a machinist and Army veteran, but he was much more than those titles and occupations. He was an investment broker into the life of his nephew, who needed a strong male figure in his life. For that I will always be grateful.

11 *The Temperature Has to Be Just Right* **The Furnace of Leadership Development**

"There is no royal road to learning; no short cut to the acquirement of any art."

— Anthony Trollope, Novelist

Anthony Trollope captures two ideas easily applied to leadership development: artwork and the road we must travel. Although scientific and human behavior principles apply, leadership is an art. Unless you purchase a paint-by-numbers Mona Lisa or a dot-to-dot picture book, any complicated form of artwork requires a lengthy road of learning. This chapter explores the two concepts of leadership development as an art, and as a highway where a toll is required.

A PRECIOUS GIFT

One Christmas morning in the mid-1990s, my wife gave me a carefully wrapped gift. Even though the box weighed approximately the same as a book, the present was far too small to be one. As I tore the wrapping paper in pieces, my wife told me to be careful. Filled with curiosity and anticipation, I opened the lid of the small box. Wow! Inside I found a glass paperweight measuring approximately three inches in diameter, with flowers of glass inside the creation. I admired the five azure blue flowers, each with intricately formed petals surrounding a clear bubble in the center. The petals taper into an elaborate white ovary and receptacle, surrounded by white and clear leaves at the base of the paperweight.

I cherish the gift not only because my wife gave it to me, but also for the sentimental family ties to glass manufacturing.

The paperweight was not made on a machine. Nor was it made in a kiosk at the local mall where glass artists fabricate small animals, flowers, and other objects. My gift was painstakingly formed by a craftsman, a glass artist at the Wheaton Arts and Cultural Center, formerly known as Wheaton Village, in Millville, New Jersey. Among the attractions is a replica of the glass factory constructed by T.C. Wheaton in 1888. For many years, Wheaton Glass was one of the primary employers in Cumberland County. My great-grandfather and other family members and friends worked in the large factory complex. Some of them worked in the "hot end" where molten glass was injected into molds, producing various shapes and sizes of bottles.

Wheaton Village opened in 1968 and I enjoyed visiting as often as possible. When I was on leave from the military, I would often watch the artists at work in the replica factory. After my wife and I married, I made a point to take her there to watch the artists make paperweights and other pieces of elaborate glass art.

THE GLASS FURNACE

The lava-like, molten glass is kept at temperatures between 2,100 to 2,400 degrees Fahrenheit inside a large furnace. Small iron doors open on the furnace to reveal a hot, bright, orange-red glow. The artist uses a gathering iron approximately four feet in length to collect the liquefied glass. At this point, the glass is roughly the size of a softball.

The artist dips the hot glass into granulated colored glass and reinserts the rod into the furnace. After the gathering iron is removed, the paperweight is shaped by various water-soaked wooden tools. When the hot glass contacts the wet apple wood or cherry wood shaping tools, charcoal is formed, which in turn polishes the glass. During this phase of the process, the rod is continually turned to prevent the glob from falling off or changing shape.

The flower is created by pouring finely powdered glass into a pattern mold. After gathering more glass from the furnace, the artist presses the rod into the mold. Throughout the process, the rod is returned several times to the furnace and the glass undergoes further shaping and polishing.

When work on the paperweight is completed, the glass ball must be removed from the rod. This is a crucial time, as the glass could easily break. After the glass has sufficiently cooled, the artist uses a scissors-like tool called a pucella to make a cut near the steel rod. The paperweight is cracked off the gathering iron and set inside a specially designed box for up to forty-eight hours to cool.

In 2014 my wife arranged a one-hour session at a glass studio in Loveland, Colorado, as a birthday present. I'd wanted to do this on our visits to Wheaton Village, but could not due to time constraints. The hour spent at the Loveland glass studio was a unique and fun learning experience for both of us, and we are now the proud owners of three hand-crafted glass paperweights. The one from Wheaton Village is perfectly round with flowers inside, while the two my wife and I made resemble jellyfish, minus the tentacles.

THE FURNACE OF LEADERSHIP DEVELOPMENT

Why is there a difference in quality between the paperweights? The two resembling jellyfish were made by rank amateurs with less than an hour of teaching and training. Whereas the Christmas gift was crafted by an individual who spent years perfecting the necessary skills to make a beautiful piece of art. The artist's ability to skillfully work with hot, molten glass did not happen overnight. It came about after years of dedicated hard work. Likewise, in order to develop as leaders, we must devote time and effort to mold and shape our skills. This requires commitment, determination, perseverance, patience, and a willingness to learn.

The temperature of the glass must stay within a workable range throughout the process of making a paperweight. If the artist leaves the gathering iron inside the furnace too long, the glass melts and ultimately falls off the rod. Conversely, if the glass cools too rapidly, it may shatter into hundreds of shards. The same principle applies to our leadership development. Too much heat and we melt into a useless blob. Too cold and we cannot be molded. The temperature has to be just right in order to properly form and develop as a leader.

Hard-charging, highly motivated individuals often take on too much responsibility too soon. Sometimes, the heat increases slowly, and the new leader doesn't even feel the temperature rising. Very much like the analogy of boiling a frog. Place the amphibian in a pot of cold water, slowly increase the heat, and the frog gradually adjusts to the temperature of the water. However, when the water reaches 212 degrees Fahrenheit, the frog is cooked. The same applies to eager and energetic leaders, like Sally in the following hypothetical example.

As a star basketball player in high school, Sally struggled with her grades but devoted countless hours to practicing the game. She dreamed of playing the sport on the United States Olympic team. However, in her senior year she suffered a shoulder injury, ending her pursuit of a gold medal. In college Sally buckled down in class, worked hard on a degree in finance, and graduated with honors. Throughout high school and college, Sally worked well with small teams and rose to the top as a leader in her groups.

After college Sally accepted a position in the accounting department for the large aerospace corporation, Wings in the Sky. It didn't take long for her boss, Fred Frugal, to recognize Sally's potential. She became the supervisor of a small work group. As opportunities arose to work on various projects, Sally volunteered to take them on. She also decided to pursue a master's degree. Fred knew Sally was a go-to person so he enrolled her in a week-long leadership seminar taught by renowned leaders from around the world.

However, over time, Sally began to withdraw from work and her colleagues. She no longer volunteered to work on projects and became annoyed when extra work was assigned to her. Sally's job performance slipped, and her subordinates recognized a disturbing change in her behavior. Sally's attitude became apathetic and she lost interest in work and in leadership self-development. What happened? Sally took on too much, too soon, and she became overwhelmed with responsibility and obligations.

Situations like Sally's are all too common, but avoidable with wisdom and forethought. Proverbs 23:12 reads, "Apply your heart to instruction, And your ears to words of knowledge." Leadership growth involves accepting challenges stretching us beyond our comfort zones. However, we should not stretch too far and cross the fine line between competence and incompetence. Sally required a proper mixture of heat from the furnace and the cool application of water-soaked shaping tools in order for her to mature as a leader without shattering. A leadership development plan could have saved Sally's job, credibility, and sanity (the concept of planning is explored later in the chapter).

THE LEADERSHIP HIGHWAY

You may recall Trollope's quote at the beginning of the chapter: "There is no royal road to learning." Neither is there an easy road to leadership development. Along the way there are many challenges and obstacles, but we have a choice to enjoy the trip or make it miserable for ourselves.

One of the most beautiful and scenic routes in the United States is California State Route 1 south of Monterey. As my wife and I traveled along the road, people sped by us, weaving in and out of traffic, in a hurry to get someplace. A few miles south of Carmel, our car topped a hill. As we rounded a curve, a stunning, awe-inspiring vista appeared before our eyes. The dark blue waters of the Pacific Ocean were contrasted against a lighter blue sky. The vegetation on the sides of the mountains had not dried out yet and the green hills were dotted with colorful red and yellow flowers. For as far as we could see, the white, foamy waves of the ocean crashed on the rocks below the road. The scene before us was the jaw-dropping, majestic creation of God. Was the trip worth it? You bet it was! And your leadership development is worth it even when people seem to speed by, and the road twists and turns.

In the 1970s, I was assigned to Seymour Johnson Air Force Base in Goldsboro, North Carolina, and frequently traveled between there and my home in southern New Jersey. My route selections were limited to three options, but I generally used Interstate 95.

Driving an overcrowded road came with a price, and it was more than just gasoline. For starters, the drive time averaged nine hours, unless it was the day after Christmas when the trip consumed nearly fourteen hours. The next payout literally came with toll money starting in Richmond, Virginia, and not ending until I crossed the Delaware Memorial Bridge into Pennsville, New Jersey. In between were stops at multiple tollbooths in Virginia, Maryland, and Delaware. Traffic congestion related to the volume of vehicles, construction, vehicle breakdowns, bad weather, and accidents was enough to put a person in a padded room.

My goal was to go home to southern New Jersey and I was willing to pay the toll in money, time, and traffic frustration. Arriving at the final destination, I reaped the benefits of time off, access to the Jersey shore, good food, and spending time with family and friends. Likewise, we must periodically stop to pay toll as we travel the Leadership Highway.

PAYING TOLL

Mr. Easy Street constantly looks for shortcuts and easier ways to accomplish goals. Easy Street doesn't want to pay the toll. Regardless of his egotistic opinion of himself, his subordinates are generally managed and not led. The Easy Streets I've been around do not care one iota about the people working for them. They view leadership as a control tool to obtain power, wealth, and fame. For them, the notion of developing as a leader to have a positive impact on someone else is a foreign and distasteful concept.

Mr. Easy Street exits the Laziness Highway and makes a speedy stop at the Quick Fix convenience store to purchase a bottle of leadership before resuming his travels. Entering the store, he asks the clerk, Nelson Knowledge, where the leadership bottles are. "Turn to your right and you'll find 'em at the back of the store in the cooler. They're right next to the aisle that has the books on five easy steps to becoming a trial lawyer." He thanks Nelson, pulls a sixteen-ounce bottle of leadership from the cooler, and proceeds to the checkout stand, convinced he is well on his way to the top. Easy Street hops into his shiny new car and revs the engine. The model is a Look at Me manufactured by the long-standing corporation of I'm Something Special. Speeding out of the parking lot, Easy Street doesn't pay attention to others and hits one of them on the way out. "Who was that?" he asks. "Oh well, it's probably just Joe Schmuckatelli, one of the little people in life who works for me. I have places to go and don't have time for him."

If this description fits you, it is time to stop and reassess where you are in life, why you are there, and what corrections you are going to make. The only thing at the end of the leadership shortcut is disillusionment and failure. You cannot purchase a bottle of leadership or a candy bar for fame and fortune. Frankly, people who are looking for fame and fortune rarely have any interest in leadership.

In contrast to Mr. Easy Street are the hardworking, dedicated, and conscientious individuals who are willing to pay toll and endure the hardships of the trip. Recently, my friend and his wife made a round-trip drive between Colorado and several locations along the East Coast. The excursion not only cost them in fuel, lodging, and food, but they paid over $100 in toll money. You must ask yourself if you are willing to pay toll and withstand the leadership challenges often encountered on the highway of life.

Challenges are opportunities for growth. Also, each stop along the leadership toll road requires time: time you invest in your own development along with time devoted to others. More often than not, you will sacrifice time that could have been spent on hobbies or sports. However, a word of caution must be inserted: do not sacrifice your family or health in order to develop as a leader. You must set priorities and properly allocate your day, week, month, and year. You will also pay a financial toll for leadership development through the purchase of books and subscriptions, seminars and classes, and picking up the tab for coffee and food when meeting with others. It is well worth paying the toll for leadership development, and you will avoid the disillusionment associated with taking shortcuts.

MAPPING YOUR LEADERSHIP ROUTE

I have enjoyed the topic of geography since youth. I love reading maps and looking at globes. My Mom-Mom (grandmother, for people outside of South Jersey) subscribed to *National Geographic*. I looked forward to reading each new issue filled with beautiful photographs of exotic locations far away from New Jersey. I was thrilled to remove the multicolored maps and charts accompanying many of the issues. To this day, I still use and prefer paper maps to digital.

In order to develop as leaders, we must map the route and not rely on someone else to drive us to the destination. You must put forth the time and effort to design a realistic plan. There are added benefits if you are fortunate to work for an organization or boss that helps with your development.

In the military, leadership development came by way of formal schools and courses. However, I was out of the military for ten years before my organization allowed me to go to an officer development course at the Rocky Mountain Fire Academy in Denver. I took the initiative to search out the class, submit a request to attend, and then justify it to my superiors. It is hard for me to believe now, but our fire department did not provide any type of internal leadership training at the organizational level until 2009. That's when we hired a chief who believed in developing the leadership capabilities of people. The key word to grasp is "initiative," because you cannot rely on your organization or anyone else to develop you as a leader.

There is a Civil War battlefield in Bentonville, North Carolina. If we want to visit the field and study the leadership of Union General William T. Sherman during the fight, we have to start by asking a couple of important questions. How do we get to Bentonville and what is our overall goal? The same maxim applies to your leadership development. Where do you want to go as a leader and how do you want to get there? Determine what you want your leadership to look like. Long before any house or building is constructed, an architectural rendition and floor plan are completed. The builder would be a fool to say, "I hope everything turns out all right." Hope is a good thing, but it is not a plan of action.

THE IAP OF LEADERSHIP DEVELOPMENT

As previously mentioned, an IAP is an incident action plan. For the majority of emergencies I respond to in my role with the fire department, the IAP is verbally transmitted to the resources assigned to the incident. I track their actions and the progression of the incident on a tactical worksheet. For more complex incidents or large-scale planned events, it is necessary to develop a written IAP. Standardized forms developed by the Federal Emergency Management Agency are used nationwide. A cover sheet generally contains a logo, organizational emblem, or a photo from the incident. Forms cover the incident briefing, objectives, assignment, communications plan, medical plan, and an activity log. This type of planning is absolutely necessary to bring organization and order to chaotic situations. In the absence of an IAP, there will be confusion, disorganization, and a haphazard approach to ending the emergency.

Likewise, we need to plan for our own leadership development. Over four years ago I was introduced to a man I have come to know and respect, Paul Callan. Paul is a retired Marine Corps colonel who owns and operates a leadership development program called The Callan Course. During a phone conversation in 2015, Paul challenged me with a question I wished had been posed to me much earlier in life. He asked, "Rick, why do you believe what you do about leadership?" Throughout all of my studies, training, college courses, reading books, and talking to mentors, I had never been asked that question before.

Two months prior to the conversation with Paul, our command staff had attended a twelve-hour leadership seminar designed to help us determine our purpose in life. I believed my purpose was based on service to others for Jesus Christ. I was and still am rooted in the second part of Luke 12:48 ("to whom much has been committed, of him they will ask the more"). The prework for the class mapped a timeline of my life and identified high points, low points, and watershed events. The exercise also included pinpointing people who positively influenced my life over the years. I went to the neighborhood coffee shop under the mistaken notion that I would only think of about five people.

After two hours my list contained fifty-two names! I was shocked at who I remembered and what impact they had on my life.

Homework in hand, I marched off to class, still under the impression that I knew what my purpose in life was. After all, I was in my late fifties, and if I didn't know by that point then I must be one screwed-up guy. During the next day and a half, we listened to each other's stories and completed additional exercises related to our personal values. These were coupled with our strengths, gifts, talents, and abilities. We also identified our passions, callings, and desired legacies. The result was a written purpose statement. I was correct about my purpose in life, but now it was in writing and read: "To impact others by leading and teaching."

After Paul's question about my beliefs on leadership, I returned to the coffee shop with a Moleskin journal and wrote "LEADERSHIP" in the upper left-hand corner. That was June 2015, and since then I have a journal filled with names, experiences (good and bad), and lessons learned. The first page lists my core virtues, gifts, and talents identified during the April seminar. I also added to my purpose statement, which now reads, "To impact others by leading and teaching, and to bring glory to God." On the next page, I listed what I believe are the characteristics, qualities, and virtues of leadership. On separate pages I wrote three questions:

- What is my motivation for leading?
- What is unique about my message and viewpoint?
- What is leadership?

The answers to those questions became the foundation for my leadership philosophy. Before you begin work on your leadership action plan, I recommend you do the same. The exercise helps to define your leadership philosophy and your present capabilities as a leader.

DEVELOPING A LEADERSHIP ACTION PLAN

As an incident commander I must first understand the situation facing me before I can develop an incident action plan. This does not mean every fact or piece of information is known. Attempting to gather that much data will lead to analysis paralysis.

In the context of the leadership action plan, you need to ask yourself questions to appreciate the situation you are facing.

- What is my leadership philosophy?
- What characteristics and qualities do good leaders possess?
- What is my current leadership position and who am I influencing?
- What type of leadership training have I received?
- What leadership books and articles have I read?
- Do I associate with credible leaders who can help me with my development?
- What gaps exist in my leadership development?

The answers to these questions will provide a better understanding of where you are with your leadership development and help define your strategy. Also, later in the plan you will use the answers to help define your tactical approach. For now, let's look at strategy because that drives the plan.

At the scene of an emergency, I begin my mental IAP based on visual observations and radio traffic. Every incident action plan contains a strategy which is the broad picture of what needs to be accomplished. When fighting structure fires, we use one of two strategies. Offensive strategy indicates we are going to aggressively attack the fire from inside the building in a safe and sane manner. We declare a defensive strategy when the fire has consumed so much of the building that we cannot safely put anyone inside.

The strategy for my leadership action plan is to impact others by leading and teaching, and to bring glory to God. Ask yourself, "What do I want my leadership to look like?" This also means you must know what core values you possess. These values are so important you will not compromise them under any circumstance, even if it means losing your job. These qualities may include integrity, faith in God, responsibility, truthfulness, trustworthiness, honesty, loyalty, justice, etc. Find a quiet spot and write down everything you can think of, creating a list of qualities you believe good leaders possess. Circle the top ten core values. Finally, narrow that list down to the five core values you will not compromise under any circumstances.

Let's return to the example of the structure fire. If the incident commander declares an offensive strategy, then everyone understands the fire is attacked from the interior of the building with the goal of confining the fire to the room or floor of origin. Once the strategy is announced, then the concepts and methods engaged to fight the fire are referred to as tactics. However, before addressing the tactical components of a leadership development plan, let's look at important foundational principles.

FOUNDATIONAL PRINCIPLES OF LEADERSHIP

Professional tactics are built on sound principles and practices, not haphazard experiments. Take responsibility for your leadership development and do not walk around in a world of bewilderment. Develop your tactics on a firm foundation. In Matthew 7:24-27, Jesus spoke of the "wise man who built his house on the rock." When the rain, wind, and floods came, the house withstood the onslaught. In comparison, the foolish man "built his house on the sand" and it did not survive the pounding weather. In I Corinthians 3:11 Paul said, "For no other foundation can anyone lay than that which is laid, which is Jesus Christ." He is the best foundation to build upon.

Wisely build your leadership development tactics around character. Proverbs 9:1 tells us, "Wisdom has built her house, She has hewn out her seven pillars." Although the Bible does not specifically identify what the seven pillars of wisdom are, I believe the following list is a good place to start.

1. Fear of the Lord – Proverbs 9:10
2. Knowledge – Proverbs 10:14 and 15:7
3. Instruction – Proverbs 1:3 and 9:9
4. Understanding – Proverbs 14:33
5. Learning – Proverbs 1:5
6. Discretion – Proverbs 3:21
7. Wisdom – Proverbs 4:7-9

The Apostle Peter lists eight characteristics in II Peter 1:5-7 that easily rest on the above pillars. He wrote, "But also for this very reason, giving all diligence, add to your faith virtue, to virtue knowledge, to knowledge self-control, to self-control perseverance, to perseverance godliness, to godliness brotherly kindness, and to brotherly kindness love." Take close note of the words Peter used in this passage of Scripture, beginning with diligence. In order for a leadership action plan to work, we must be diligent to act, otherwise we will spin our wheels in the mire of procrastination. Peter's use of the word faith is applied to faith in Jesus Christ. He's not speaking of faith in ourselves, faith in the government, faith in a financial institution, or faith in anything else other than Christ.

The word interpreted as "virtue" in our Bibles is the Greek aretē meaning "whatever procures pre-eminent estimation for a person or thing; hence, intrinsic eminence, moral goodness, virtue."[37] In 1828, Noah Webster defined virtue as bravery, valor, and excellence; "or that which constitutes value and merit."[38] Among other qualities, successful leadership requires bravery, valor, and excellence. Peter also highlighted knowledge, self-control, and perseverance. In today's electronic age, knowledge is readily available and often easily obtained. However, self-control and perseverance require a determined effort on our part. The last three qualities in the passage are godliness, brotherly kindness, and love—three important elements woefully absent in our society. In the passage of Scripture from II Peter 1 mentioned earlier, the apostle said "add to." The sum of these qualities is a person of integrity with unquestioned character—a description of the ideal leader for your family, friends, subordinates, employer, church, and nation.

FINAL STEP: DEVELOPING YOUR TACTICS

In the section about Developing a Leadership Action Plan, I listed seven questions to assist with defining your strategy. The last question was: What gaps exist in my leadership development? Until you identify those areas, you are flying blind, and you will have no idea of what you need to work on for improvement. Once you honestly pinpoint the gaps then you are ready to develop the tactics.

Tactics are the concepts, methods, and techniques employed to accomplish the mission. In other words, tactics describe how the job will be carried out. However, it is imperative for you to understand that the tactics I speak of require you to dig deep into your soul. It is not an easy to-do checklist of items nor is it the magic elixir that cures leadership deficiencies. This is *your* leadership plan involving hard work and effort on *your* part to develop character. Just as firefighting involves action, so does your plan.

Return to your favorite quiet spot and identify the tactical actions required to accomplish your strategy. As you refer to the previous list of questions, answer the following:

- What characteristics and qualities do I need to improve to be a good leader?
- How can I better influence those I lead and impact?
- What type of leadership training do I need and where can I get it?
- What leadership books should I read?
- What are other credible leadership resources I can use?
- What credible leaders can I associate with to help me develop as a leader?
- Who will provide honest and constructive feedback to help me grow as a leader?

Relative to the last two questions in the list, seek out a mentor. I guarantee there are people willing to help you develop your plan and help you see it through. They may not be readily apparent and it may take some footwork on your part to find them. In the original *Star Wars* movie, Luke Skywalker went to great lengths to seek Yoda for help in becoming a Jedi warrior. Proverbs 24:6 aptly states, "For by wise counsel you will wage your own war, And in a multitude of counselors there is safety." Remember that although there are scientific and human behavior principles involved in working with people, leadership is an art. And developing an artistic talent requires hard work, dedication, perseverance, study, and practice.

Practical Application

- We must experience the heat of the furnace in order to be pliable and molded. However, the temperature must be just right or we will either melt from the heat or shatter in the cold.
- As we travel the Leadership Highway, we must periodically stop to pay toll. This comes in the form of invested time and effort in our development.
- The leader who fails to personally develop will fail to develop other people.
- Map your route and develop a leadership action plan.
- Build upon the foundation of Jesus Christ described by Paul in I Corinthians 3:11. On the foundation erect the seven pillars of wisdom and add the eight characteristics listed in II Peter 1:5-7.
- Leadership is an art requiring time, effort, and hard work on our part.

Time to Leave the Firehouse

"We mistakenly think of leadership as if it were a coat;
something we put on at 8 a.m. and take off at 4 p.m.
For leaders that coat never comes off!"

— Paul Callan, Colonel, United States Marine Corps (Ret.)

In the Preface, I invited you to sit with me at the firehouse kitchen table, drink coffee, and listen to my experiences and perspectives on leadership. Our time at the table is finished and we have reached the end of the book, but not the end of your development as a leader—hence the reason I did not use the word "conclusion." The moment a person chooses to conclude their development as a leader is the moment a person decides to hang their leadership coat in the closet. Then what happens to the coat? It becomes old, dusty, and moth-eaten. Useful to no one. I purchased a coat in the mid-1990s and still wear it during cold weather. Why has the coat lasted so long? Because I believe in caring for my investments. I wash and clean the coat, and periodically treat the fabric with a product to enhance the water repellant capabilities of the material. Likewise, we must care for our leadership coat.

Throughout the book, I have been transparent and laid bare some of my leadership failures and hard-learned lessons. I, too, have struggled as a leader, but have grown as a result. For your sanity and peace of mind, it is important to realize you are not alone when dealing with leadership problems.

Be very careful who you compare yourself to, as that generally does nothing but create problems for us. We may look to others as good examples and desire to emulate their leadership style and methods. But never forget that you have a unique set of gifts and talents and a personality that enhances your leadership ability.

Leadership is hard and not always an easy, smooth road. The weak will not survive the furnace of testing and they will melt into the crowd. They are the ones nobody wants to work for or be around. Take advantage of your time in the furnace and allow yourself to be molded into a better leader. Even during the periods of difficult shaping, take the time to look out for those who are entrusted to your care. Do not be afraid to ask questions in order to gain better clarity and to grow as a leader. Demonstrate the courage to ask and do not become a slave to fear, as you will be no good to anyone. Asking questions requires a humble spirit, which means we must slay our egos.

Never forget that leadership is not associated with a title, rank, or position of authority. Leadership involves the people in our lives. Our families, spouses, loved ones, friends, coworkers, subordinates, casual acquaintances, and others we encounter on a daily basis.

Never forget your integrity. It is the foundation for successful leadership. Regardless of academic records, physical attributes, career achievements, or charisma, if someone lacks integrity, they are dishonest charlatans. Through your integrity, you not only gain the trust of others, but you will experience open doors of opportunity awarded to people of strong character. Writing in I Timothy 6:20, the Apostle Paul said, "O Timothy! Guard what was committed to your trust . . ." Wise words to apply in our lives.

As you take the last sip of coffee and prepare to leave the firehouse, remember what we have talked about. Leadership is composed of integrity, trust, credibility, determination, and physical and moral courage. Leadership involves listening, consistency, justice, and equity. These and other qualities come into play when we deal with organizational monsters, intra-team conflict, bias toward others, and providing and receiving feedback. An important component of leadership is self-control over anger and negative emotional responses. How we handle disappointment, rejection, and failure also impacts our leadership of others. Leaders are decision-makers and have the ability to function in an environment of chaos. Another significant element of leadership involves our personal development.

Finally, invest one of your most precious commodities into the lives of people: your time. The return on investment brings long-term rewards and the personal satisfaction of knowing that you are impacting their lives. Lay aside any selfish desires and lead those who are entrusted to your care. Push forward and persevere. Determine to be the leader who others want to imitate.

Although you have reached the end of the book, the door to the fire station is always open. You are invited to return as often as possible to the firehouse kitchen table. We can drink a cup of coffee, talk about the adventures of Joe Schmuckatelli, and learn more about leading people. And *NEVER* forget that the key to leadership is *people.*

Acknowledgments

The writing and publication of this book spans a two-year period and was accomplished with a capable team. A heartfelt thank you is extended to each one. Susie Schaefer of Finish the Book Publishing for her encouragement, guidance, and wisdom. Polly Letofsky of My Word Publishing for encouraging me to start writing the book and for her business acumen. Nick Zelinger for the fantastic cover design and patience working with me through the selection process. Chelsea Hoffman of Easely Inspired for the logo accurately portraying our dog Java. Last but not least in this category is my editor and writing coach, Alexandra O'Connell. I am forever grateful for her candid feedback and work on the manuscript. Furthermore, she understands my Jersey sense of humor and is a fan of Joe Schmuckatelli, one of the characters in the book.

Thank you to Paul Callan for challenging me to dig deep and discover the roots of my leadership beliefs. Appreciation is also extended to the men of Cedarville Fire Company No. 1, New Jersey, for allowing a teenager to hang around the firehouse and eventually join their ranks in 1976. I'm grateful for the U.S. Air Force firefighters who helped shape my career. Thank you to the U.S. Marine Corps for opening my eyes to what true leadership is. Thank you to the former and current members of the Loveland Fire Rescue Authority, Colorado, for allowing me to be a part of your life and share my leadership experiences at the coffee table. Many of you encouraged me to write a book and pass on the lessons I learned in life to others.

The experiences described herein cover a lifetime of learning and involve many people too numerous to mention. I want to thank those who are named within the pages of the book who contributed in a positive manner to my development as a man, member of the military, firefighter, and leader. Although many events were painful at the time, I'm thankful for the opportunities I had to go through the furnace of leadership development.

The three remaining team members are my family. Thank you to Debbie, my beautiful wife of thirty-two years who has stood by me in both the good and bad times. I thank God for her love, support, and encouragement. Although Debbie doesn't physically ride in the command vehicle with me, I know she prays for me each and every day. She has laughed with me when I tell her about the funny firehouse stories and she comforts me when I share the tragedies associated with firefighting. Rebekah and Emily are blessings from God and they are beautiful, encouraging, and supportive daughters. All three provided input during the writing process. May God richly bless you.

Psalm 30:12 sums up my thanks to God for His help and guidance: "To the end that my glory may sing praise to You and not be silent. O Lord my God, I will give thanks to You forever."

Notes on the Chapter Epigraphs

Chapter 2

Trust is the glue of life. Covey, Stephen R. *The 8th Habit: From Effectiveness to Greatness* (New York: Free Press, 2004), 162.

Chapter 3

The way out of trouble. Grothe, Mardy. *Metaphors Be With You: An A-Z Dictionary of History's Greatest Metaphorical Quotations* (New York: Harper, 2016), 403.

Chapter 5

To be a critic. San Antonio *Current.* "Judith Crist (1922-2012), pioneering film critic: An appreciation," August 8, 2012, https://www.sacurrent.com/ArtSlut/archives/2012/08/08/judith-crist-1922-2012-pioneering-film-critic-an-appreciation.

Chapter 6

Anger is momentary madness. Grothe, 24.

Chapter 8

Defeat is simply a signal to press onward. Grothe, 102.

Chapter 9

A good solution applied with vigor. Province, Charles M. *Patton's One-Minute Messages, Tactical Leadership Skills for Business Managers* (Novato, CA: Presidio Press, 1995), 21.

Chapter 10

Someone's sitting in the shade today. Rule One Investing, "50 Warren Buffett Quotes on Investing, Life & Success," accessed June 27, 2018, https://www.ruleoneinvesting.com/blog/how-to-invest/warren-buffett-quotes-on-investing-success/.

Chapter 11

There is no royal road to learning. Grothe, 236.

Time to Leave the Firehouse

We mistakenly think of leadership as if it were a coat. The Callan Course, accessed January 9, 2019, www.callancourse.com.

Endnotes

Chapter 1

1 U.S. Marine Corps. *The Marine Noncommissioned Officer,* Marine Corps Institute, Marine Barracks, Washington, D.C.

Chapter 2

2 United States Department of Commerce, "Performance of Structures During the Loma Prieta Earthquake of October 17, 1989," January 1990, accessed November 3, 2017, http://ws680.nist.gov/publication/get_pdf.cfm?pub_id=908823.

Chapter 4

3 Statista, "Sources of stress at work reported by employees in North America as of 2017," accessed June 20, 2019, https://www.statista.com/statistics/315848/employee-stress-sources-at-work-in-north-america/.

4 Mayo Clinic, "Stress symptoms: Effects on your body and behavior," accessed June 20, 2019, http://www.mayoclinic.org/healthy-lifestyle/stress-management/in-depth/stress-symptoms/art-20050987.

5 Michael Blanding, "Workplace Stress Responsible for Up To $190B In Annual U.S. Healthcare Costs," *Forbes,* January 26, 2015, https://www.forbes.com/sites/hbsworkingknowledge/2015/01/26/workplace-stress-responsible-for-up-to-190-billion-in-annual-u-s-heathcare-costs/#f128198235a2.

6 Goodwin, Doris K, *Team of Rivals: The Political Genius of Abraham Lincoln* (New York: Simon and Schuster, 2005).

7 Hewitt, William D, *The Campaign of Gettysburg: Command Decisions* (Gettysburg, PA: Thomas Publications, 2012), 75.

8 Keneally, Thomas, *American Scoundrel: The Life of the Notorious Civil War General Dan Sickles* (New York: Doubleday, 2002).

9 Sifakis, Steward, *Who Was Who in the Union, Volume I: A Biographical Encyclopedia of more than 1500 Union Participants* (New York: Facts of File, Inc., 1988).

10 Hewitt; Peatman, Jared, "General Sickles, President Lincoln, and the Aftermath of the Battle of Gettysburg," *The Gettysburg Magazine* 28 (2003), Morningside House, Inc., Dayton, OH: 117-123.
11 Pfanz, Harry W, *Gettysburg, The Second Day* (Chapel Hill, NC: The University of North Carolina Press, 1987) 429.
12 Loveland Fire Rescue Authority, "About Us," accessed June 20, 2019, https://lfra.org/about-us/about-us/.
13 McCoy, BP, *The Passion of Command: The Moral Imperative of Leadership* (Quantico, VA: The Marine Corps Association, 2006), 54.
14 McMichael, Alford L, *Leadership: Achieving Life-Changing Success from Within* (New York: Simon and Schuster, 2008).
15 Patterson, Karry, Joseph Grenny, Ron McMillan, and Al Switzler, *Crucial Conversations: Tools for Talking When Stakes are High* (New York: McGraw-Hill, 2012).
16 Gray, Al and Paul Otte, *The Conflicted Leader and Vantage Leadership* (Columbus, OH: Franklin University Press, 2006), 121.

Chapter 5

17 Mendte, Larry, "7 Ways to Tell If You're a Shoobie," *Philadelphia Magazine*, May 24, 2019, https://www.phillymag.com/news/2010/05/24/7-ways-to-tell-if-youre-a-shoobie/.
18 Lyons, Fran, *The Loveland Fire Department: The First 125 Years* (Loveland, CO: Loveland Museum and Gallery, 2017).
19 Thomas Jefferson Foundation, Inc, accessed June 20, 2019, https://www.monticello.org/site/research-and-collections/i-never-considered-difference-opinion-politicsquotation.
20 Grothe, 409.

Chapter 6

21 Team Building and Event, "Team Building Quotes by Zig Ziglar," November 7, 2013, http://www.tbae.co.za/blog/team-building-quotes-zig-ziglar/.
22 RBC Ministries, Grand Rapids, MI, 1982.
23 American Psychological Association, "How to Recognize and Deal with Anger," accessed February 10, 2018, www.apa.org/helpcenter/recognize-anger.aspx2018.
24 KeepInspiring.Me, "115 Thomas Jefferson Quotes on Life, Government, and Religion," accessed June 20, 2019, www.keepinspiring.me/thomas-jefferson-quotes.
25 Giglio, Louie, *Goliath Must Fall: Winning the Battle Against Your Giants* (Nashville, TN: HarperCollins Christian Publishing, Inc., 2017).

Chapter 7

26 Claudio Fernández-Aráoz, "21st-Century Talent Spotting," *Harvard Business Review*, June 2014, https://hbr.org/2014/06/21st-century-talent-spotting.

27 Tougias, Michael and Casey Sherman, *The Finest Hours: The True Story of the U.S. Coast Guard's Most Daring Sea Rescue* (New York: Scribner, 2009).

Chapter 8

28 Covey, Stephen R, *The 7 Habits of Highly Effective People* (New York: Simon & Shuster, 1990), 237.

Chapter 9

29 Snowden, David J. and Mary E Boone, "A Leader's Framework for Decision Making," *Harvard Business Review*, November 2007, 68, https://hbr.org/2007/11/a-leaders-framework-for-decision-making.

30 Trudeau, Noah A, *Gettysburg: A Testing of Courage* (New York: HarperCollins Publishers, Inc., 2002), 413.

31 Davis, Richard W, "Making Rapid Tactical Decisions Under Stress," National Fire Academy, Emmitsburg, MD, 2010.

32 Davis, Richard W, "Situational Awareness at the Command Level," National Fire Academy, Emmitsburg, MD, 2012.

Chapter 10

33 National Coffee Association USA, "The Economic Impact of the Coffee Industry," accessed June 27, 2018, http://www.ncausa.org/industry-resources/economic-impact .

34 The Independence Hall Association, "The Electric Ben Franklin: Drive the Bridge," accessed June 20, 2019, http://www.ushistory.org/franklin/philadelphia/bridge.htm.

35 *Foundations Magazine*, "George Washington's Rules of Civility & Decent Behavior in Company & Conversation," accessed July 5, 2018, www.foundationsmag.com/civility.html.

36 Grothe, 180.

Chapter 11

37 Vine, WE, *Vine's Expository Dictionary of New Testament Words* (McLean, VA: MacDonald Publishing Company, 1940), 1212.

38 Webster, Noah, ed., *American Dictionary of the English Language*, original 1828; republished 1995 by Foundation for American Christian Education, San Francisco, CA.

About the Author

Battalion Chief Rick Davis currently serves as a shift commander with the Loveland Fire Rescue Authority (LFRA) in Colorado. He has been in the fire service for over thirty-six years and with LFRA for twenty-nine. Rick is the leader of the LFRA Special Operations Team, and has served as leader of the LFRA hazardous materials team, wildland firefighting program, and was the department's training chief. Rick is a veteran of both the United States Air Force and United States Marine Corps.

Over the course of his career, Rick has spoken about and taught leadership and decision-making to fire service, industry, and church groups. He wrote two research papers on situational awareness and tactical decision-making under stress. Rick earned a bachelor's degree in Business Administration from Kennedy Western University, a master's degree in Executive Fire Service Leadership from Grand Canyon University, and is a graduate of the National Fire Academy's Executive Fire Officer Program.

Originally from Cedarville, New Jersey, he now lives in Loveland, Colorado, with his wife, Debbie, two daughters, Rebekah and Emily, and their dog, Java. Rick is a student of leadership and military history, and finds studying the Gettysburg Campaign of 1863 of great interest. He enjoys the Atlantic Ocean and walking Civil War battlefields. To invite Rick to speak at your event or organization, please contact him at Info@ImpactusLeadership.com.

As a military and fire service veteran, Rick Davis, founder of **Impactus! Cultivating Today's Leaders,** brings over 40 years of leadership experience to guide you through solving your organization's challenges through leadership coaching. Rick's passion for helping others comes through by leading, teaching, and training professionals to create "fired up" teams that get results. Impactus! services include:

- Leadership presentations & training
- Full- or half-day seminars & workshops
- One-on-one leadership coaching & mentoring
- Facilitating group discussions & problem-solving

Please email Info@ImpactusLeadership.com for availability, pricing, and to schedule your complimentary 30-minute consultation.